THE LUCKY **SHOPPING** MANUAL

building and improving your wardrobe piece by piece

the Lucky shopping manual

building and improving **your wardrobe** piece by piece

KIM FRANCE AND ANDREA LINETT

EDITED BY DANIELLE CLARO

ILLUSTRATIONS BY SYDNEY VANDYKE

GOTHAM
BOOKS

MELCHER
MEDIA

To Eve France and Caryl Linett, the coolest moms on the block,
whose great senses of style remain our strongest inspiration.

THIS BOOK WAS PRODUCED BY MELCHER MEDIA, INC., 124 WEST 13TH STREET, NEW YORK, NY 10011. WWW.MELCHER.COM

Gotham Books Published by Penguin Group (USA) Inc. 375 Hudson Street, New York, New York 10014, U.S.A.; Penguin Books Ltd, Registered Offices: 80 Strand, London WC2R ORL, England; Penguin Books Australia Ltd, 250 Camberwell Road, Camberwell, Victoria 3124, Australia; Penguin Books Canada Ltd, 10 Alcorn Avenue,Toronto, Ontario, Canada M4V 3B2; Penguin Books (N.Z.) Ltd, Cnr Rosedale and Airborne Roads, Albany, Auckland 1310, New Zealand.

PUBLISHED BY GOTHAM BOOKS, A MEMBER OF PENGUIN GROUP (USA) INC.

First Printing, October 2003 10 9 8 7 6 5 4 3 2 1 Gotham Books and the skyscraper logo are trademarks of Penguin Group (USA) Inc. ISBN 1-592-40036-1 Printed in China

CONTENTS

Long before we had our own magazine, we used to sit around and talk about how cool it would be to do a book. We imagined helping women effortlessly overcome the most basic (and therefore the most baffling) style quandary: How do I get dressed in the morning? We wanted to show real women how to put together realistic, truly chic looks with the clothing already hanging in their closets (or shoved in the hamper), while also inspiring them to go out and shop. The book we dreamed of writing would be populated—at least in an inspirational sense—by women with great style, women who could toss on a T-shirt and jeans and instantly look appealing and sexy and smashing. Our book would also be chock full of helpful style hints that we'd culled from particularly fashionable shop girls, pointers we'd picked up at photo shoots, and ideas we'd spied on the street. It would be the *Joy of Cooking*, but of shopping and style, and we hoped it would become just as dog-eared, tattered, and loved.

But—and this thought never ceases to amaze—instead of doing a book, we got to launch a magazine. And with *Lucky*, we've been given the opportunity to do so much of what we had wanted to do with that book. Every month, we get excited all over again to show readers page upon page of clothing and accessories that we're really, truly worked up about. Although *Lucky* does show readers how to put all of this together, there are only so many pages in the magazine to do so.

So now that our dream of making a book has come true, we have some general points of advice on how we think it should best be used. Unlike in *Lucky*, there's nothing in this book that you can explicitly buy. Instead, use the *Manual* to help you make outfits with all the things you already own (and also to help you out when it's time to shop). This book is full of advice on everything from the most flattering shoe to wear with cropped pants to precisely how a jacket should fit over a dress. And while we think we've pretty much nailed it, you might not always agree. So if you find that, contrary to our observations, a cap-sleeve T-shirt is not the most flattering shape on your arm, don't follow our advice. Finally, we will be devastated if the *Manual* sits pristinely in your living room collecting dust along with a bunch of high-concept design volumes and an expensive candle from France. Like *Lucky* magazine itself, this book is meant to be read, tossed in your bag, consulted, re-consulted, marked up, and generally trashed.

We hope you enjoy digging into the *Lucky Shopping Manual* as much as we did thinking about it and talking about it and generally obsessing over it for the past ten years. Our hope is that you keep referring back to it, season after season, and that it continually gives you new answers and better solutions. We can assure you that this book won't go out of style at the end of winter 2003 or spring 2005 or whenever. It's around for the long haul, and it'll always be there to help out.

Kim and Andrea

CHAPTER 1

SKIRTS

PLEATED

PENCIL

PLAID

TIERED

LEATHER

FLORAL

SEQUIN

ASYMMETRICAL

A-LINE

DENIM

SUEDE

CIRCLE

fit and styling tips

1 FLATTER LEGS

A skirt that hits the widest part of your calf can make legs look shorter and thicker, giving you a dowdy look. To solve the problem, hem the skirt to hit mid-knee. With the top taper of the calf revealed, legs look longer and shapelier; the total effect is cool instead of frumpy.

2 FOOTWEAR AND LEATHER SKIRTS

Keep leather skirts away from leather boots. Try pumps or T-straps instead. If you want to wear boots with your leather skirt, go with a suede pair. The reverse works too: combine a suede skirt with leather boots, but skip the suede + suede combo.

too much leather

just right

3 HOW TO WEAR A LONG SKIRT

The exact right length is critical here: A long skirt should just *almost* touch the floor. Drapey long skirts should be especially fitted through the hips, so your shape doesn't get lost in all that fabric. Don't wear heels with long skirts unless it's for evening. For daytime, stick with refined pointy or plain-toe flats that just peek out the front of the skirt.

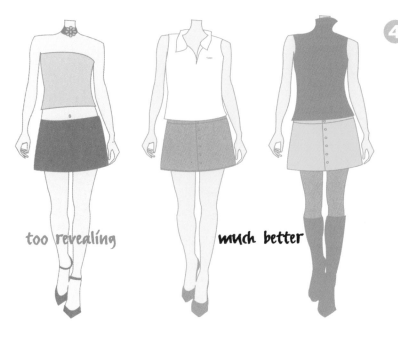

too revealing   *much better*

④ LOOK COOL, NOT TACKY, IN A MINI

A miniskirt runs the risk of looking tarty. Keep it sleek instead by countering its inherent sexiness. Choose a top that's on the tame side—nothing skintight or terribly revealing—and footwear that follows the same principle. In winter, a flat knee boot is perfect, with or without tights. In summer, ballet flats give that chic French-girl effect. Keep the look modern with a mini that sits low on your hips, not right on your waist. And, by all means, steer clear of heels.

⑤ SHOW SOME SKIN FOR A LEANER LOOK

When you're wearing a straight skirt with boots, always reveal some leg in between (bare skin or dark tights, whatever you prefer). Closing up this space can make your legs look stumpy, especially with stiffer boots. When you show the line of your actual legs—even only a couple of inches—the problem is solved. A flared or full skirt with boots can look right with no leg showing at all, as long as the boots are fitted through the ankle. One boots-and-skirts policy that applies across the board: The boot top should always fit snugly around your calf.

more flattering

the best skirts for you

WEAR AN A-LINE SKIRT IF YOU WANT TO...

(A-LINE SKIRTS LOOK GREAT ON EVERYONE!)

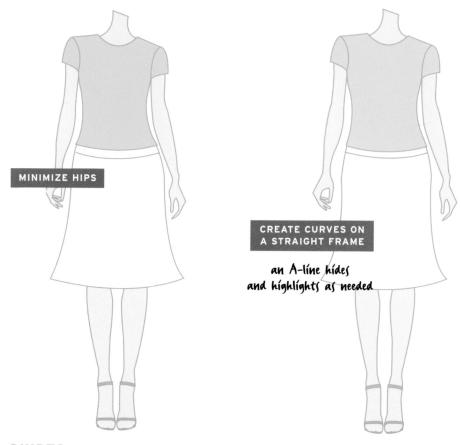

MINIMIZE HIPS

CREATE CURVES ON A STRAIGHT FRAME

an A-line hides and highlights as needed

WEAR A PENCIL SKIRT IF YOU WANT TO...

SHOW OFF YOUR SHAPE

LOOK CURVIER

the sexiest skirt there is

WEAR A LONG SKIRT IF YOU WANT TO...

LOOK TALLER

HIDE THICK LEGS

even in denim, a long skirt is Cinderella-graceful

building a skirt closet

2 ALL-SEASON WORK SKIRTS
tropical wool

1 DAY-TO-NIGHT SKIRT
dress it up or down

2 SUMMER WORK SKIRTS
crisp and structured

1 DENIM SKIRT

A SUMMER EVENING SKIRT

A WINTER EVENING SKIRT

2 SUMMER WEEKEND SKIRTS

dress them up or down

A LEATHER OR SUEDE SKIRT

wear it now, wear it later

A soft wool hoodie over a suede skirt offers a cuddly contrast of textures. Complete the look with curvy leather boots.

LIGHTWEIGHT SUEDE SKIRT

SUMMER

Summer-ize suede with a vivid tee and ankle-strap espadrilles.

TIERED SKIRT

SUMMER

Pair a full cotton skirt with a fitted sexy top, and don't be shy about mixing brights and earth tones.

WINTER

When the weather's cold, a lightweight skirt can look fresh with tights, casual boots and a slouchy sweater.

3 skirts, 2 ways

WOOL SKIRT   BLACK

WORK	WEEKEND	WORK
COWLNECK SWEATER + YELLOW SATCHEL + PATENT-TRIMMED PUMPS	SHAWL NECK SWEATER + CUTOUT HANDBAG + SNAP BOOTS	PEACOAT SWEATER + STATUS BAG + SUEDE BOOTS

SATIN SKIRT

FLORAL SKIRT

SEXY SWEATER
+
FISHNETS
+
VELVET HEELS

FITTED CARDIGAN
+
BUCKLE BAG
+
RUFFLED PUMPS

POLO
+
T-STRAP SANDALS
+
ROUND-HANDLE BAG

FASHION CHALLENGE:
what to pair with a bold skirt

PLAID SKIRT

This drapey plaid wrap skirt has plenty going on, and a subdued sweater shows it off well. But you can also roll with the busy-ness by piling on another pattern; just be sure to stick with colors in the same family.

SURE...

BUT WHY NOT...

mix neutral-tone patterns

ASYMMETRICAL SKIRT

A lacy, angle-hem skirt begs for a simple black tank. But for going out at night, the fitted striped tee pulls it out of Stevie Nicks–ville.

SURE...

BUT WHY NOT...

When the skirt says so much, what can you wear on top? Instead of reaching for the safe option, try something with a bit more moxie.

SEQUIN SKIRT

A bell-sleeve tee softens the impact of a sequin skirt. But for all-out glamour, a ruffly pink top kicks it up a notch.

SURE...

BUT WHY NOT...

sexy, but not too sexy

PRINT SKIRT

A snug tank complements the fullness of this vintage-y skirt—and picks up a color from its print. But if you're feeling playful, a cute bomber jacket grooves on the retro feel and cuts a flattering hourglass shape.

SURE...

BUT WHY NOT...

defines your waist

and you're off to the nunnery

A long skirt looks old-fashioned paired with a maximum-coverage sweater. For evening, get a little sexy above the waist with a pretty sleeveless top or even a simple tank.

OTHER OPTIONS

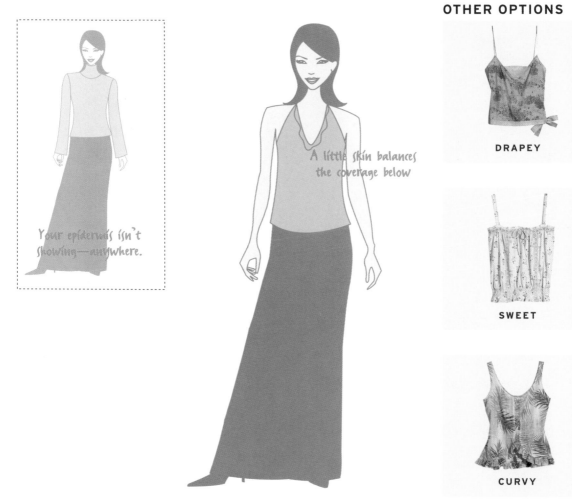

Your epidermis isn't showing—anywhere.

A little skin balances the coverage below

DRAPEY

SWEET

CURVY

IN THE FITTING ROOM

CHECK COVERAGE	Make sure a wrap skirt covers you well. If it's so spare on fabric that you can't wear it on a windy day without obsessive fear of overexposure, don't buy it.
CHANGE THE LIGHTING	Summer skirts can be unwearably sheer in backlight. Go to a brightly lit area in the store and have a friend check you from all angles.
TAKE A WALK	Even in a pencil skirt, you should be able to comfortably perform the basic motions of daily life—like walking and sitting. Leave the dressing room and stroll around the store, with a regular gait. Don't buy a skirt that forces you to teeter in baby steps or to sit with your thighs glued together.
WATCH FOR ROTATION	Slim skirts can twist, rotating slightly with each step till the side closure has worked its way around to your belly button; this can mean a skirt is too small, too large, or just not cut right for you. Try another size or style.

spend or save?

Spend on a classic-shape leather or suede skirt, or a really special evening skirt with breathtaking detail. Save on easy-to-fit casual skirts, including denim, corduroy, and wispy summerwear. There are plenty of cute options to choose from at reasonably priced stores.

LUCKY
GIRL

anne johnston albert

JOB:
DESIGNER AND
BOUTIQUE OWNER

STYLE:
PRACTICAL COOL

HER RULES...

1 "Wear well-cut modern classics that have a little edge and blend well with your own style."

2 "Clothes should be comfortable, as well as cool."

3 "Change your shoes (not your jeans) to go from casual to dressy."

DESIGNER ANNE JOHNSTON ALBERT

counts many of New York's most influential stylists and
fashion editors as devotees. They come to her cozy
East Village boutique, Martin (named after her husband), for clothes that are understated and effortlessly
cool, qualities easily ascribed to Albert herself.

Albert's look begins and ends with jeans, which are
among her signature pieces. "I throw them on with a top
and a pair of boots, and I'm dressed. I don't want to
have to think about my outfit. I don't have time."

It isn't only the normal workday commitments of running
a small business that keep Albert rushing around; her
young daughter does her part as well, and even seems
to have some effect on her mother's designs. "I'm
always bending down now—picking her up off the floor,
putting away toys—so I've added jeans with a slightly
higher rise to my line."

Also known for her drapey tops and well-cut asymmetric tees, Albert keeps things groovy but subtle. "It's
important to me that the clothes I make don't over-
power the wearer," she says. "I want them to mix with
people's style, not overwhelm it." The invisible undercur-
rent, says the designer, is practicality: "I'm constantly
trying things on to make sure they're comfortable."

VIETNAMESE PATCHWORK BAG

"I wore these with a skimpy slip dress when I got married, and they work with a pair of jeans too; basically they look good with everything."

PASHMINA

"A lightweight long-strap bag I wear across my body, so I can be hands-free running around New York."

PRADA SANDALS

"Makes everything look richer."

MY FAVORITES:

DESIGNER Dries van Noten. "His pieces are timeless—feminine but also cool."

SHOES Harness boots

JEANS Martin

HIGH-END STORES Louis Boston, in Boston. "It's very European and carries a really interesting mix of high-end designers and jewelry."

MAINSTREAM STORE K-mart, "for great cheap jewelry, simple cotton tops for layering, and men's T-shirts."

FASHION ERA Late '60s

FASHION ICON Bob Dylan and Linda McCartney (in the '60s)

COLORS TO WEAR Olive, pink, brown, navy, black, white

"I'm attracted to things that aren't too fussy. I wear this over a white tee or tank."

VINTAGE WESTERN SHIRT

GOLD BANGLES

"So easy to wear—you don't have to take them off when you get in the shower—and they make you feel exotic."

"My version of a jeans jacket."

MARTIN MOLESKIN JACKET

"The way I wear dresses is cut off over my jeans; I designed this top for that purpose."

RING

"I like things that are a little ethnic, like this hand-made roughcut-diamond ring from India."

MARTIN DAMSEL SHIRT

"The more beat up, the better."

MARTIN ASYMMETRIC TEE

HARNESS BOOTS

"The uneven bottom keeps it from falling like a big baggy old tee."

CHAPTER 2

T-SHIRTS

BOATNECK

SCOOPNECK

HENLEY

POLO

CREWNECK

V-NECK

STRIPED

BOY'S

TANK

fit and styling tips

① PERFECT FIT

It's easy to be careless about T-shirts, but a nice fit makes a huge difference: Choose tees that are tailored, rather than boxy, in not-too-thick fabrics. The shoulder seam should sit right at the widest part of your natural shoulder, and there should be no drape in the fabric under your arm. Pick a neckline that flatters you, and a length you're comfortable with. A tee that hits just at the hip always looks cool—but a longer one, provided it's body-hugging at the bottom, can be a great option, too.

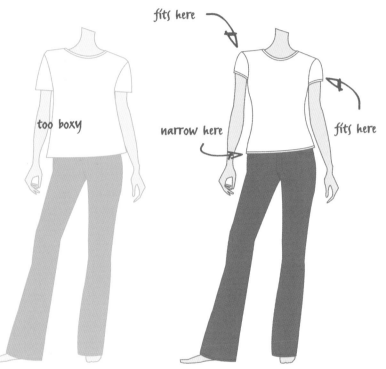

fits here

too boxy

narrow here *fits here*

② JEWELRY AND THE NECKLINE

If you feel naked without a necklace, be sure to choose tees that make room for one. A scoopneck gives you a nice wide canvas on which to work. Higher necks mean you need to move your jewelry focus. A boatneck, for example, is its own strong statement; don't wear a necklace with one. Try long dangly earrings instead.

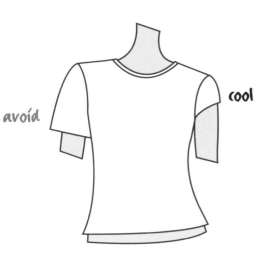

avoid

cool

③ FLATTERING SLEEVES

Cap sleeves work well on most figures, because they broaden the shoulders and make the waist look smaller. But if you prefer a little more coverage, fitted sleeves about two inches longer are fine. Avoid short sleeves that hit right in the middle of the upper arm and any sleeves that don't fit snugly. With long-sleeve tees, err on the side of extra length, with the hem of the sleeve hitting the heel of your hand.

④ RIBBED TEES

Like any kind of additional texture, ribbing tends to add bulk. To avoid this, look for tees that have fine ribbing.

⑤ HOW TO LAYER TEES

An easy way to make a statement with tees is by layering. You'll be most comfortable if your underlayer is whisper thin—a lightweight, fitted cotton tank or a silky lace-trim camisole. Throw on any tee—even those old favorites that are too short for solo use—but keep the colors of your layers in the same family. With a scrunched-up, hip-hugging tank or a bit of lace peeking out of the bottom, you achieve instant style.

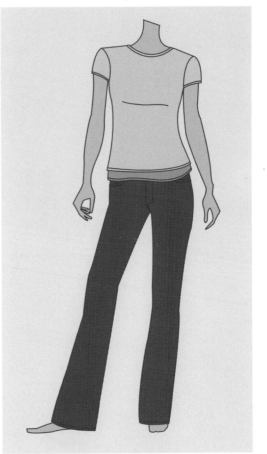

fit and styling tips

elegant but
tricky to wear

⑦ THE RIGHT BRA

Molded-cup bras, though some are advertised as "T-shirt bras," can be too thick under a thin tee. But when wearing a tee to work, a molded cup is called for; it gives you an office-appropriate, nipple-free look. A sexy option for casual wear (if you don't mind some nipple show-through) is a thin T-shirt with a sheer underwire bra; the look is very natural, and sort of '70s cool. This works best with 34B and under breasts. In either case, pick a bra with full-coverage cups—the edges of demi-cups will show through a tee.

⑥ HOW TO WEAR HIGHNECK TEES

A crewneck lends European sophistication to a casual look, but it's not for everyone. If you're big, or even medium-busted, a high-neck can make breasts appear droopy. Narrow, small to medium-breasted figures can best pull off this look. Choose a fitted tee made of cotton (no stretch), and pair it with something feminine, like slim flareleg pants and heels.

natural
look

office
tee

cuts you in half

one long line

9 SECRET TEE RESOURCE

The men's underwear department can be a great source of tees, if you know what to look for. Choose those made of a thin, springy fabric with some polyester, so they hug the body. Avoid thick neckbands, and be sure that the sleeves are very short, hitting just below your shoulder. If men's sizes are too big, check out the boys' department.

10 SEXY, BUT NOT SLUTTY

Avoid super-tight stretch tees that cling to everything you've got. A well-cut, less revealing tee is way sexier.

8 WEARING TEES WITH SKIRTS

When pairing a tee with any shape skirt, choose a tee that's snug all the way down; a fabric with a little stretch guarantees a close fit. Avoid tees that stand away from the body at the bottom, because this breaks the line of the whole tee-and-skirt shape and makes you appear shorter. For a sophisticated look, try a longer, fitted tee scrunched around the top of a skirt.

the best tees for you

BALANCE WIDE HIPS WITH...

A DEEP SCOOPNECK TEE

the open neckline broadens shoulders and lifts the focus

KEEP A BELLY COVERED WITH...

A LONGER CUT

looks cool scrunched around the hips

ENHANCE SMALL BREASTS WITH...

A STRIPED TEE

horizontal stripes work best on narrow figures

HIDE HEAVY UPPER ARMS WITH...

A BELL-SLEEVE TEE

evens the width of the arm for a long, graceful line

CONCEAL LOVE HANDLES WITH...

A LOOSER TEE IN A THICKER FABRIC

less snug, but still fitted through the shoulder and underarm

MINIMIZE LARGE BREASTS WITH...

A FITTED MEDIUM-NECK TEE

choose a longer one that won't hike up in front

building a t-shirt drawer

(2) GOOD WHITE TEES

you need a couple, because they'll stain

(2) GOOD BLACK TEES

black fades in the wash—always have a spare on hand

Choose necklines that you feel good in—even if it means all your tees are cut exactly the same.

4 TANKS

for beachwear and layering

building a t-shirt drawer

(1) STRIPED TEE

wide or narrow stripes

(1) HENLEY OR POLO

...INCE TEES ARE PRETTY CHEAP, ADD...

SOME SOLID TEES IN UNPREDICTABLE COLORS

A FEW FUN TEES

jewelry and the basic tee

Bring out the multiple personalities of a white tee with strong accessories.

UPTOWN

ELEGANT

HIPPIE

1 tee, 3 ways

WEEKEND	WORK	EVENING
PATCH-POCKET PANTS	RETRO JACKET	COCKTAIL RING
+	+	+
BEADED BRACELET	SLIM SKIRT	SATIN SKIRT
+	+	+
ETHNIC THONGS	PATENT-TRIM PUMP	EMBELLISHED SANDALS

wearing a striped tee

The clean lines of a cap-sleeve tee, jeans, and flats has a fresh, '60s charm. Add a touch of glamour with sophisticated shades.

A casual, striped boatneck brings a sporty edge to an office look. Gold hoops and red kitten heels keep the look feminine.

Horizontal stripes may have a bad reputation, but the coolness of a striped tee is indisputable. How to get away with one? Use it as the focal point of an outfit and pair it with figure-flattering neutral pieces.

This perfectly Parisian combo—classic sailor tee with a motorcycle jacket, an A-line skirt, and heels—is girly and tough at the same time.

A sexy, stretch-cotton tee and pleated skirt create a curvy figure. Sophisticated accessories make it modern.

and you're the new hire on the Starship Enterprise

A super-tight stretch crewneck has that painted-on Mr. Spock effect. If you want a sexy look, choose T-shirts with a nice neckline in rayon or cotton blends that don't stick to you like a swimsuit.

OTHER OPTIONS

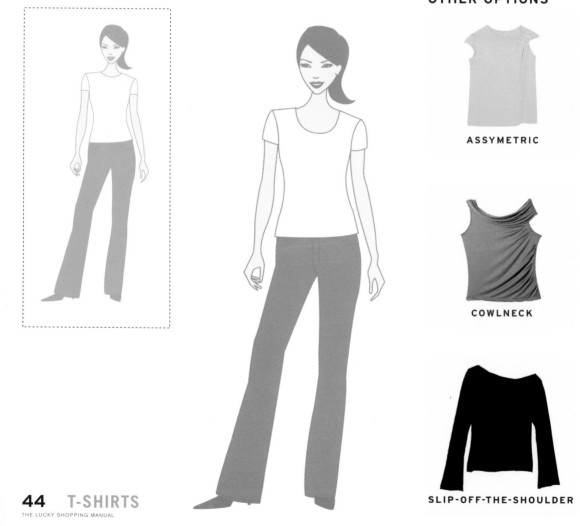

ASSYMETRIC

COWLNECK

SLIP-OFF-THE-SHOULDER

IN THE FITTING ROOM

CHECK THE NECK

U-necks or deep scoopnecks that look okay when you're upright can buckle or stand away from your body when you sit down; on some open-neck tees, even the back of the neckline has trouble lying flat. Don't buy a tee with an imperfect neckline, because you'll be tugging at it all the time.

WATCH FOR LENGTH

When you try on a tee, make sure the front isn't shorter than the back. Some tees that look right in the store are not cut to account for breasts. A bigger size might help but is probably not the solution if the tee is fitting well in the shoulders. Look for another style instead.

IGNORE THE SIZE

Don't get hung up if you discover you need to buy a tee a size or two larger than usual. Sizing can be wildly inconsistent, even at chain stores. Get the tee that looks best and that gives the effect you want, regardless of what the tag says.

spend or save?

You should be able to find tees you love without spending a lot of money. Special tees that might be worth paying extra for are silk blends with exceptionally beautiful drape or detailing. But for everyday tees, pay everyday prices—and replenish when they get stretched-out or worn-looking.

CHAPTER 3

TOPS

BUTTON-DOWN

LACE

FLUTTER-SLEEVE

SEQUIN

TUNIC

WESTERN

HALTER

OFF-THE-SHOULDER

BLOUSE

BIAS CUT

WRAP

ONE-SHOULDER

fit and styling tips

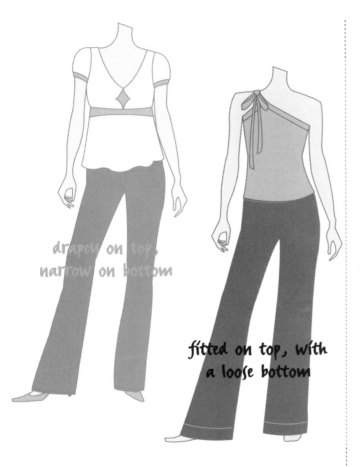

drapes on top, narrow on bottom

fitted on top, with a loose bottom

① THE TOPS-AND-PANTS FORMULA

Blousy tops look best with fitted pants or a straight skirt; a close-to-the-body top works well with a looser shape on the bottom. This isn't a hard-and-fast rule, but it's a great place to start if you're unsure about what to pair with what.

② WHAT'S SEXY IN A PARTY TOP

Dressy nighttime tops should highlight your assets, and loosely covered can be way sexier than bare or skintight. So look for tops that drape but also show off your best features. If you have nice collarbones, shop for wide necklines; pretty shoulders, find a halter top; a great back, try a backless style. Be sure you can wear your going-out tops with ease—without tugging, adjusting, or fiddling with bra straps. Looking comfortable is probably sexier than any particular style or detail.

looks elegant

too short

LENGTH CAN MAKE OR BREAK YOUR LOOK

Even the most beautiful top—one that fits well in the shoulders and is the perfect color with your hair—won't work if it's too short or too long. An over-long top cuts your legs, making them (and you) seem stumpy; a too-short top looks juvenile. Stick with tops that stop a couple of inches below the hipbone.

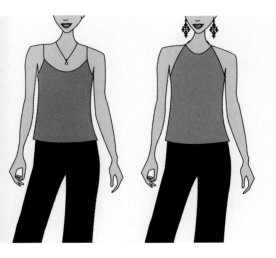

④ THE RIGHT JEWELRY

Think about both the weight and the shape of a top when you accessorize. A thin gold chain with a small pendant is perfect for a delicate party top, but heavy pearls wouldn't be right. Button-downs work best with shorter earrings, because big hoops or other long earrings can bump into the collar. Just follow the neckline: Open necks leave room for necklaces; otherwise, wear earrings instead.

fit and styling tips

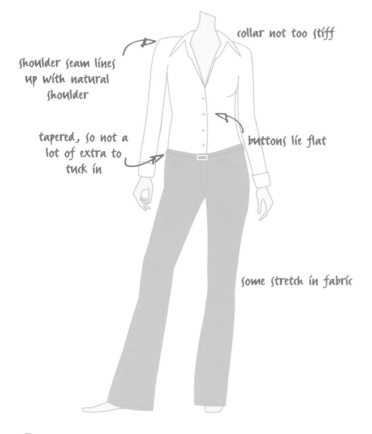

collar not too stiff

shoulder seam lines up with natural shoulder

tapered, so not a lot of extra to tuck in

buttons lie flat

some stretch in fabric

5 HOW TO NOT LOOK MANLY IN A BUTTON-DOWN SHIRT

Choose a cut that tapers to fit your curves, not one that's loose and boxy (avoid the paper-bag effect). Ideally, the fabric will have some give; a bit of stretch helps the shape. The perfect fit is tailored through the shoulders without pulling across the chest.

6 SHOPPING FOR PARTY TOPS

Work tops need to be relatively tame and practical. But party tops are the dessert of your wardrobe, so go ahead and indulge. Look for details that make a top special, like ties, lace, or little embellishments. Be adventurous, and try on styles you might normally skip; you have a little latitude because you'll be wearing these tops at night, in low light. That said, keep your eyes peeled for shapes you know work, and don't fall for a trend that doesn't flatter you.

7 WHEN DOES IT WORK TO UNTUCK

A silk or rayon blouse with a tailored bottom can go untucked and still look clean and professional as long as it hangs above the hip bone. Most button-downs made of cotton shirting are meant to be tucked in. For a casual look, a button-down with a shaped hem worn out can work with jeans.

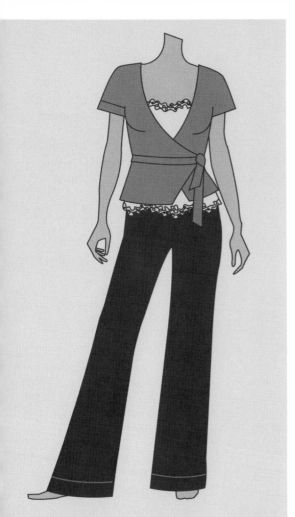

9 FIT AND THE TAILOR

Little adjustments can improve the fit of some tops, but there are certain requirements a top should meet at the store. For example, the shoulder seam should fall in the right place; nothing should be pulling; and your breasts should be located where they're meant to be. Good candidates for alterations are tops that need simple shortening work—spaghetti straps, sleeves, overall length. A tailor can also narrow a too-wide top, but keep in mind that a delicate fabric, like chiffon, may carry an extra fee for alterations.

be sure the seam falls where it should

8 RECYCLE SPECIAL TOPS

Party tops can be trendy, and last season's must-have item might seem all wrong this year: too short, too boxy, just somehow off. But don't give it away just yet: Try a thin tank or cami underneath, and see what you can come up with. A lace-trim camisole under a short, pretty top can make for a cool—and totally individual—going-out look.

the best tops for you

ENHANCE
SMALL
BREASTS
WITH...

DISGUISE
A THICK
MIDDLE
WITH...

MAKE **NARROW**
SHOULDERS
BROADER
WITH...

A STRETCHY TOP WITH
GATHERING AT THE BUST

A TOP WITH A BUILT-IN
TAPERED WAIST

A RACER-BACK SHAP[E]

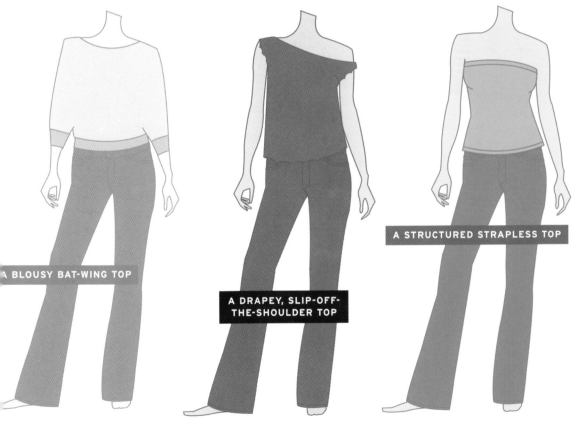

HIDE **HEAVY ARMS OR LOVE HANDLES** WITH...

SOFTEN **TOO-WIDE SHOULDERS** WITH...

COMPLEMENT **LARGE BREASTS** WITH...

A BLOUSY BAT-WING TOP

A DRAPEY, SLIP-OFF-THE-SHOULDER TOP

A STRUCTURED STRAPLESS TOP

building a top closet

6 WORK TOPS

your choice of shapes

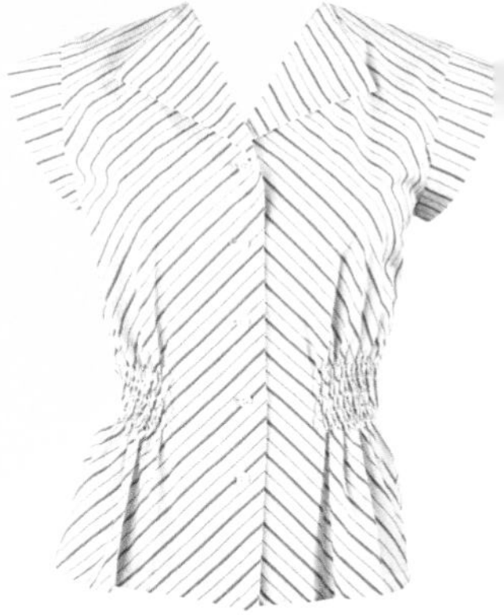

3 FUN TOPS

for going out at night

4 WEEKEND TOPS

t-shirt alternatives

building a top closet

BECAUSE TOPS CAN TRANSFORM A WHOLE OUTFIT, ADD...

MORE FUN TOPS

because you can never have too many

FASHION CHALLENGE:
what to wear with a fabulous top

Jeans are dependable with pretty tops, but a neutral yet interesting skirt or pair of pants still allows a special top to shine.

A zippered pencil skirt toughens up this ruffly lace top.

This stretch sequin top becomes more casual with summery white canvas pants.

A sexy juxtaposition of masculine and feminine; pinstripe trousers with a floaty chiffon top.

3 work tops, 2 ways

SILKY BLOUSE

PRIN*

WITH PANTS	WITH A SKIRT	WITH JEANS
SHAPED SUIT + **TWO-TONE SLINGBACKS**	**PLEATED COTTON SKIRT** + **POINTY MULES**	**JEANS** + **ANKLE STRAPS**

*the mules
make it sexy*

WITH A SKIRT

FULL TWEED SKIRT
+
JEWELED THONGS

WITH PANTS

TAB-FRONT TROUSERS
+
SEXY PUMPS

WITH A SKIRT

CRISP MINI
+
PIPED FLATS

both sexy and demure

pick your favorites

CAP SLEEVE

MANDARIN COLLAR

VINTAGE-Y

WORK TOPS

PINTUCKED

CAMP SHIRT

JOHNNY-COLLAR

FLUTTER-SLEEVE

CAMISOLE

BELTED

FUN TOPS

EMBROIDERED MESH

SEQUIN

SATIN

wear it now, wear it later

An eyelet top dresses up for summer with white trousers, strappy sandals, and a lightweight cardigan.

EYELET TANK

WINTER

For winter, a suede skirt, leather boots, and a safari-style jacket give this sweet top a bit of an edge.

WINTER

This graphic-print silk blouse is the soul of an edgy winter work look, with collar and cuffs peeking out from beneath a thin sweater.

SUMMER

Worn open over an all-white tank and jeans, this bright, light piece adds the perfect shot of color to a casual summer outfit.

SILK BLOUSE

and you're in Donna Summer's "Bad Girls" video

Don't go overboard, even when dressing up. Balance the sexiness of a sequin top and shoes with the classic charm of a full skirt.

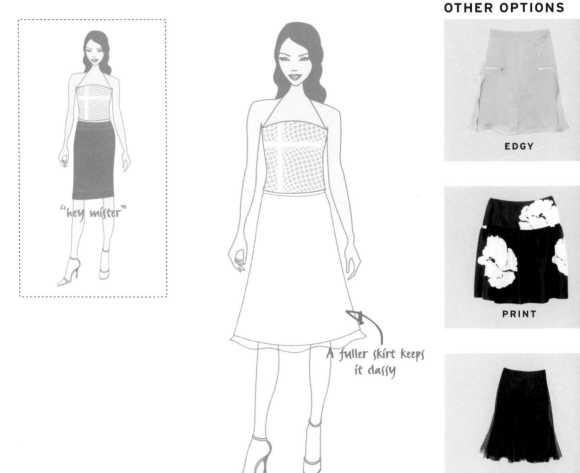

"hey mister"

A fuller skirt keeps it classy

OTHER OPTIONS

EDGY

PRINT

RUFFLE

IN THE FITTING ROOM

TRY **THE BUTTONS**

Sometimes the second button on a button-down shirt is placed too high; it looks frumpy closed, but it reveals too much left open. When shopping for shirts, wear a low-front bra (demi-cup or front closure) so you can check this. Ideally, you'll find one that buttons just low enough to barely cover your bra—which makes for a flattering open neckline.

SIT **DOWN**

Stretch button-downs that look right when you're standing can buckle across the chest or ride up when you sit or slouch. Try a larger size, but don't sacrifice shoulder fit. Skip the shirt if you have to; you shouldn't buy one that needs to be tugged down every time you change positions.

TUCK **IT IN**

Avoid shirts made of a too-stiff fabric that balloons out when tucked. Also pay attention to the amount of fabric that needs to be tucked; too much can add bulk to your waistline.

spend or save?

Spend on the tops you wear to work—rich materials and good tailoring can really step up an office look. Save on party tops, which tend to be passionate (as opposed to practical) purchases. Shop inexpensive chains, where tops are cute and trendy, and even check out the juniors department. It's better to spread out your budget over a few cheaper fun tops than to dump it all into one pricey piece.

miguelina gambaccini

JOB:
CLOTHING DESIGNER

STYLE:
ROMANTIC SENSUALIST

HER RULES...

1 "Bring out your inner beauty with graceful, feminine pieces that make you feel comfortable with yourself."

2 "Keep it simple at night: A great dress, heels, and a bright shawl."

3 "A drapey top or dress with a pretty neckline is sexier than something tight."

"I ADMIRE WOMEN with a very strong sense of style, someone like Frida Kahlo," says Dominican-born Miguelina Gambaccini, a designer of deliciously lush clothes, who splits her time between Tuscany and New York.

Just as you instantly recognize a Kahlo painting, you know a Miguelina dress when you see it: silky, sexy, feminine, in a startlingly deep hue. It's no surprise that Gambaccini's personal style is at the core of her professional aesthetic: "I design things I'd like for myself," she says. "I'm constantly creating my wardrobe—what I'd want to wear on a trip, to a cocktail party, relaxing in my garden."

Inspired by the bohemian spirit of her Spanish heritage, the romance of the Victorian era, and the richness of nature, Gambaccini's own pieces define her look and comprise almost her entire wardrobe. For running around doing business in New York, she might wear a bright lace-trim silk top with jeans; at night, a charmeuse dress and heels ("definitely heels!"). In country mode (she designs at her home in Tuscany), Gambaccini is all about lightness: a longer linen slip-dress, handmade leather sandals, and a vivid shawl tucked in her bag are all she needs.

Gambaccini not only dresses romantically, but she also lives the part; candles, roses, and introspection are all essential to her creative process. "To me, style is the way you feel inside, projected through clothes," she says. "I don't think a woman has to wear something tight to look good. Instead, clothes should bring out the beauty within."

from miguelina's closet

GARNET CROSS NECKLACE

"I collect crosses. This one's an antique Spanish colonial, given to me by my husband."

GAUZE SHAWL

"I always take this with me when I travel. I reminds me of the ocean."

MIGUELINA CHARMEUSE CAFTAN

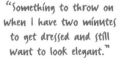

"Something to throw on when I have two minutes to get dressed and still want to look elegant."

MY FAVORITES:

DESIGNER "I only wear the clothes I design, but I like Petit Bateau T-shirts."

SHOES "Manolo Blahnik, the sexiest, most feminine shoes—and they're also comfortable. For daytime, sandals from Leather Villa or flip-flops.

JEANS Alvin Valley

HIGH-END STORES Prada, for bags

MAINSTREAM STORE J. Crew, for T-shirts

FASHION ERA "Turn of the last century, through the '30s. And I love the '50s."

FASHION ICON Coco Chanel

COLOR TO WEAR White, "especially in summer"

ANTIQUE BEADED BAG

"Perfect for a party. I love the '20s feel."

"I love this with jeans for daytime."

MIGUELINA BLOUSON CAMISOLE

MIGUELINA CHARMEUSE BLOUSE

"I call this my adira blouse—in Spanish, adira means girly, in a sexy way."

MIGUELINA LINEN DRESS

"Nice over a swimsuit for the beach"

CHAPTER 4

DRESSES

SHIFT

VINTAGE

HALTER

SUNDRESS

FLORAL

LITTLE BLACK

WRAP

SLIPDRESS

STRAPLESS

fit and styling tips

① WEARABLE VINTAGE SHAPES

A '40s-style frock is easy to wear because it broadens the shoulders and drapes gracefully (thanks to a bias cut). But dresses with full skirts—more of a '50s look—are a double whammy for all but the narrowest figures; the fitted bodice makes the upper body tiny and the hips, by comparison, big—and gathering at the top of the skirt bulks up the waist.

makes hips bigger

flattering

② GET SERIOUS ABOUT WORK DRESSES

While skirts can be versatile, morphing from casual to professional with the change of a top or shoes, a dress is distinctly what it is, and usually occupies only one category. Work dresses should be refined. Whether tailored or A-line, they should have simple, elegant lines. Save dresses that are unstructured or floppy for the weekend.

work

weekend

③ LABEL LOYALTY

Dresses are unusually tricky, because they have to fit well in so many different spots: shoulders, bust, waist, hips, and length. So, if there's a label or boutique whose dresses fit you well, stick with it. And if you find a near-perfect dress that needs minor adjustments, by all means, buy it and have it altered.

④ CHANGE THE BRA, NOT THE DRESS

Shaped dresses can require a certain amount of assistance from undergarments. If your breasts are not lining up with the darts in the bodice of the dress, a more supportive, molded-cup bra could make a difference.

⑤ ACCESSORIZE AGAINST TYPE

Use jewelry to balance the strong personality of a dressy dress—you don't want to be too match-y or you run the risk of looking like you're in costume. Make a sweet party dress a little more sophisticated with big, sexy hoops. Add bold, silver jewelry to a shirtdress to keep it from looking uniform-ish. Just be sure to keep accessories in synch with the dressiness of your dress. If you wear a watch, choose a delicate watch rather than a chunky one, and carry an evening bag instead of your everyday bag.

cinch at the hip to give a formless dress shape

⑥ REVITALIZE A DRESS WITH A BELT

Any dress that doesn't have its own shape—from a shirtdress to a slipdress to a vintage schmatte—can benefit from a belt. Look for a curved belt, because straight versions can ride up, and consider the fabric of the dress; a delicate slipdress needs a lighter-weight leather or maybe even a fabric belt. If you have a dress hemmed, save the piece that's taken off the bottom: it can work as an obi-style sash, so the dress remains one color, but curves in where you need it to.

the best dresses for you

MINIMIZE HIPS WITH...

CREATE A WAIST ON A STRAIGHT FRAME WITH...

ACCOMMODATE A CURVY FIGURE WITH...

A NEAT A-LINE

A SHAPED SHIFT

A WRAP DRESS

it's adjustable

FILL OUT SLOPED SHOULDERS WITH...

FLUTTER SLEEVES

HIDE HEAVY ARMS WITH...

SHEER OVERSLEEVES

covered, but still sexy

LOOK TALLER WITH...

AN EMPIRE WAIST

wear it now, wear it later

A black cotton dress goes to work with spicy T-straps, a classic coat, and a clever tote.

SUMMER

BLACK DRESS

In summer, add strappy sandals and a fun bag, and this versatile dress is evening ready.

It's right for the office with bright kitten-heel slingbacks and a sharp carryall.

WINTER

With equestrian boots and a peacoat, it's an easy winter weekend piece.

BLACK DRESS

building a dress closet

YOU'RE TOTALLY COVERED FOR SUMMER IF YOU HAVE...

2 WEEKEND DRESSES

1 EVENING DRESS

1 DAYTIME PARTY DRESS

2 WORK DRESSES

IF YOU'RE A GIRL WHO LOVES DRESSES, ADD...

the most comfortable thing to throw on when it's sweltering

MORE SUMMER WEEKEND DRESSES

building a dress closet

1 WEEKEND DRESS

2 WORK DRESSES

1 EVENING DRESS

IF YOU'RE A GIRL WHO LOVES DRESSES, ADD...

for all the holiday parties

MORE WINTER EVENING DRESSES

pick your favorites: summer

CREPE

PRINT

SHIRTDRESS

RETRO

LIGHT DENIM

KEYHOLE

GEOMETRIC

GATHERED

WEEKEND DRESSES

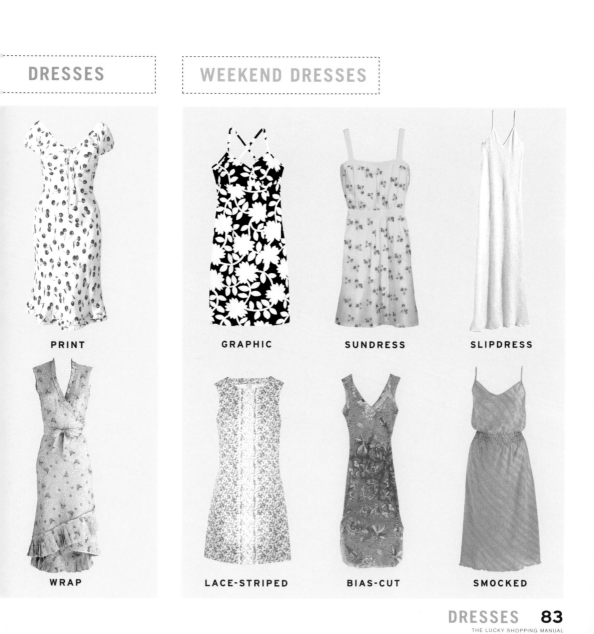

PRINT

GRAPHIC

SUNDRESS

SLIPDRESS

WRAP

LACE-STRIPED

BIAS-CUT

SMOCKED

pick your favorites: winter

BELTED

PINSTRIPE

TULLE

BOUCLÉ

TWEED

DRAPEY

HANDKERCHIEF HEM

WOOL JERSEY

EMBROIDERED

WRAP

FULL

GATHERED

choosing shoes

**FLORAL SLIPDRESS
+
STRAPPY SANDALS**

**LACE OVERLAY DRESS
+
SATIN PUMPS**

The gold gives it a funky '80s feel

**CHIFFON DRESS
+
METALLIC SANDALS**

T-SHIRT DRESS
+
LEATHER THONGS

COTTON VOILE DRESS
+
PRETTY PUMPS WITH DETAILING

MESH-OVERLAY DRESS
+
EMBELLISHED SLINGBACKS

the sexy shoe makes the dress less sweet

earthy meets sporty for weekend

ONE FALSE MOVE...
and you're the maid of honor

Fight the urge to match the color and vibe of your dress and shoes. Balance the neat lines of a sculpted dress with a slightly wilder strappy sandal, and the look is more evening than wedding party.

OTHER OPTIONS

I hope I catch the bouquet

A little skin

CLASSIC

SEXY

TOUGH

IN THE FITTING ROOM

SIT DOWN

Because it covers so much of your body, a dress is radically affected when you sit down; you might suddenly discover that a shift is too snug, a party dress is too poufy, or a sexy dress is actually closer to obscene. In a tailored dress made of a stiffer fabric, look for a fit that doesn't change much when you sit. The top should stay put, not hike up, and the neckline should lie flat, not stand away from your body.

DANCE

If you're shopping for a party dress, be sure it can handle the activities you intend it for, while not overexposing you. So move a bit, reach your arms up, lean forward, and see where it lands. The last thing you want is to get out on the dance floor and then realize you made the wrong choice.

SEEK PROFESSIONAL HELP

As you check out a dress's fit, keep your mind open to visiting the tailor. Straps, sleeves, and hemlines are generally not a problem to alter. A tailor can also narrow the waist of most dresses. But if you have to make too many adjustments to a dress, it may not be the wisest purchase. And though tailors are great at making things smaller, they can't do much in the other direction; for example, a shift that's tight across the butt can't be fixed with alterations.

spend or save?

Spend on tailored winter work dresses, because a great fit is a necessity; an ill-fitting shift looks sloppy and adds pounds. Save on casual, unstructured summer dresses, which exist in a realm where quantity might actually be more important than quality. Between sun, salty air, and sweat, flimsy summer dresses are often trashed by the end of the season. So buy cheap and get more than one.

CHAPTER 5

SWEATERS

SLOUCHY

CARDIGAN

V-NECK

VEST

CREWNECK

ZIPPER

VINTAGE

CHUNKY

TURTLENECK

fit and styling tips

 PERFECT FIT

There's nothing neater or more elegant than a skinny crewneck sweater that fits the way it should. Look for shoulder seams that line up with your own natural shoulder, sleeves that gently hug your arms all the way down, and a shape that's narrow through the waist and hip. No matter what your figure, avoid boxy sweaters; close-to-the-body cuts are more modern and more flattering.

fits here and here

narrow here

SAVE SHRUNKEN SWEATERS

A cardigan or pullover that's too short to wear on its own (a washing machine casualty or a once-trendy shorter cut) can work well as part of a casual layered look. Pull it on over a longer underlayer with detailing that peeks out of the bottom, like a camisole or printed T-shirt. Be sure to keep your underlayer thin, so you don't add bulk.

HOW TO WEAR A SWEATER OVER A BUTTON-DOWN SHIRT

A great combo, but you must proceed with caution. A stiff cotton shirt under a sweater can look conservative or mannish—not to mention bulky, with lots of fabric wrinkling beneath the sweater. Instead, opt for a silky, slim-fitting, button-down (solid or patterned) that will lie smooth. Choose a fitted sweater in a dark color (you don't want any show-through), but not one that's so tight and thin that it reveals the outline of buttons and bumps underneath. A deep scoopneck sweater can look good with the shirt unbuttoned low. Another option, if you like the clean line of a collar without layers: A sweater with a polo collar—or a trendier style with built-in collar and cuffs.

too bulky

slouchy but sexy

LOOKING GOOD IN AN OVERSIZE SWEATER

The trick here is to make sure your shape isn't swallowed up inside a big, formless sweater. Choose a soft, drapey knit, which will conform to your arms and show your shape a bit. And don't buy too big. Watch shoulder seams, too: They won't fall on your natural shoulder in an oversize sweater but they shouldn't be too far off, or you run the risk of adding pounds.

CAREFUL WITH COLORS

The sweater department can yield soft pastels that tempt you toward a palette you might otherwise avoid. Candy colors are less classic, so they can make for a risky sweater purchase. If you're investing in an expensive sweater such as cashmere, you can't go wrong with subtle sophisticated neutrals like black, navy, brown, camel, or gray.

WORK WITH THE NECKLINE

Don't wear a necklace with a sleek high-neck sweater—dress it up with long earrings instead; style boatnecks and turtlenecks similarly. Sexier necklines, like a scoopneck and a deep V leave room for necklaces or a glimpse of a pretty camisole underneath.

the best sweaters for you

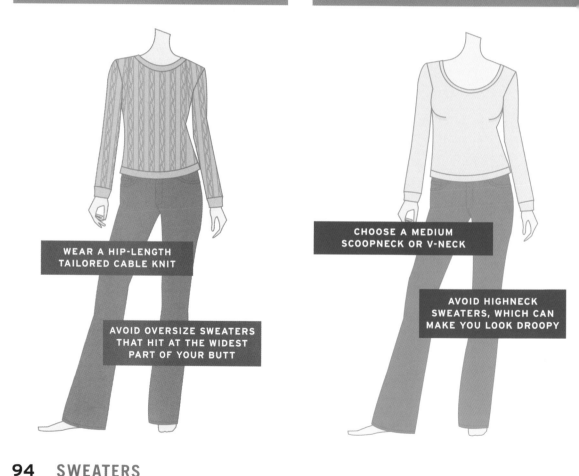

IF YOU'RE PEAR-SHAPED...

WEAR A HIP-LENGTH
TAILORED CABLE KNIT

AVOID OVERSIZE SWEATERS
THAT HIT AT THE WIDEST
PART OF YOUR BUTT

IF YOU'RE BIG-BUSTED...

CHOOSE A MEDIUM
SCOOPNECK OR V-NECK

AVOID HIGHNECK
SWEATERS, WHICH CAN
MAKE YOU LOOK DROOPY

IF YOU'RE VERY TINY...

WEAR FITTED PULLOVERS AND CARDIGANS SCALED TO YOUR SIZE

AVOID BIG, SLOUCHY SWEATERS THAT SWALLOW YOU UP

IF YOU HAVE LOVE HANDLES...

CHOOSE STYLES THAT ARE FITTED UP TOP BUT STAND AWAY FROM THE BODY AT THE BOTTOM

AVOID SWEATERS WITH WIDE RIBBING AT THE WAIST

building a sweater closet

YOU'RE TOTALLY COVERED IF YOU HAVE...

2 CARDIGANS

for evening and office

2 FITTED PULLOVERS FOR WORK

v-neck or crewneck

1 BLACK TURTLENECK

thin and fitted, not boxy

IF YOU'RE A REAL SWEATER GIRL, ADD...

*sexy, whether vintage
or slouchy*

AN EVENING SWEATER

fun and trendy

(2) **WEEKEND
SWEATERS**

at least one that's truly warm

MORE WEEKEND
SWEATERS

ONE VINTAGE SWEATER

GETTING DRESSED:
3 sweaters, 2 ways

V-NECK

CREW

SLEEK

PLAID TROUSERS
+
PATENT-LEATHER PUMPS

SEXY

SILVER NECKLACE
+
FLARE-LEG JEANS
+
HARNESS BOOTS

SLEEK

PEARL STUDS
+
PRINT SKIRT
+
CUT-OUT PUMPS

V-neck leaves room for a little jewelry

TURTLENECK

SEXY

TURQUOISE EARRINGS
+
LOW-RISE JEANS
+
METALLIC SLINGBACKS

SLEEK

SLIM CARGOS
+
CHARM BRACELET
+
KITTEN-HEEL PUMP

SEXY

CHUNKY RINGS
+
SATIN MINISKIRT
+
BUCKLE BOOTS

FASHION CHALLENGE:
wearing tricky sweaters

LONG CARDIGAN

This potentially overwhelming style tends to work better for weekends and evenings than for work. Try the casual rustic charm of a long cardigan with jeans, or juxtapose it with a wispy dress for an unexpected going-out look.

SURE...

BUT WHY NOT...

CLASSIC CARDIGAN

Worn open, a cardigan can look matronly—but it actually becomes slick when it's all buttoned up. Pair it with slim black pants for a sophisticated silhouette, or make it sizzle with a skin-baring mini.

Balance the shape of hard-to-wear sweaters with pieces from the other end of the spectrum: Big goes with little, nubby goes with silky, and prim goes with sexy.

SLOUCHY SWEATER

To wear an oversize sweater without feeling dumpy, make sure everything from the waist down is slim. Narrow pants are an easy option, but a body-slimming slip dress works too.

SURE...

BUT WHY NOT...

SWEATER VEST

A striped sweater vest is both cool and classic over a white button-down. But with a tiny tee and slim skirt, it gets a little edgy.

SURE...

BUT WHY NOT...

and you're the dowager aunt

A twinset is the picture of proper: Perfectly matching and entirely covered up. For some sex appeal, pair it with a pencil skirt to counter its primness.

OTHER OPTIONS

A little leg goes a long way

IN THE FITTING ROOM

CHECK THE RIBBING

A narrow band of ribbing at the bottom of a classic pullover can look good, but make sure it doesn't pull the sweater in and create a blouson effect. Ribbing shouldn't interrupt the line of the sweater; instead it should function as a continuation of the shape. The same applies to ribbing at the cuffs and neck—a narrow band looks cool and polished, but anything that messes with the drape should be avoided. Unless that's the specific shape of the sweater.

EVALUATE THE ITCHINESS

It's easy to fall in love with a sweater that looks amazing and to numb your body to the discomfort you're experiencing while gazing at your fabulously transformed self. The best way to judge how something feels opposed to how it looks is to minimize irrelevant sensory input. In other words, get away from the mirror. Don't buy an itchy sweater no matter how great it looks; you'll never wear it.

spend or save ?

Putting a big chunk of your sweater budget toward a good cashmere sweater is better than owning a heap of mid-quality pieces. It's the one you'll reach for time and again when getting dressed for work. Save on weekend sweaters by opting for cotton or inexpensive acrylic blends that simulate (to amazing effect) soft, natural fibers.

carlota espinosa

JOB:
TV REPORTER

STYLE:
BUSINESS WITH
PLEASURE

HER RULES...

1 "If you have to think about whether an outfit works, don't bother with it; dressing should be easy."

2 "Do trends, but always with classics."

3 "Save your splurges for great shoes, great bags, and excellent tailoring—they elevate your whole look."

AS A PRODUCER of TV style segments in Los Angeles, Carlota Espinosa is constantly surrounded by the latest trends (not to mention the red-carpet-bound celebrities who often spark them). To keep above the fray, Espinosa relies on clothes that are dependably chic. "My philosophy is keep it simple," she says. "Don't get caught up in trying too hard."

Clean, shapely suits provide polish when she needs it. "You look instantly pulled together in a well-cut suit, no matter what the environment," says Espinosa. And, she adds, "it gives your confidence a boost."

To those who fear all businesswear is staid, she recommends shopping around for flattering shapes, "and definitely add your own personality. I'll wear a bright camisole under a suit for a burst of color, or a patterned top to give it an edge."

At times when a suit is too much, Espinosa opts for blazers. "I own a range of styles, from classic to funky—but always fitted." She'll wear them with slim trousers and flats (she's 5'9") and grab accessories on her way out the door. "I might twirl a scarf around my neck or add earrings, but I do it impulsively," she explains. "If I think about it too much, it takes the fun out of dressing."

from carlota's closet

KATAYONE ADELI SPARKLY TANK

"My perfect shoe."

SIGERSON MORRISON HEELS

"I wear this with a corduroy blazer for work; for evening, I lose the blazer and add heels."

WOOL PANTS

"My favorite pants. They're part of my work uniform, and also nice for evening because they have a sexy fit."

MY FAVORITES:

DESIGNER Marc Jacobs

SHOES Sigerson Morrison

JEANS Blue Cult, Earl Jean

HIGH-END STORES Barneys New York, Henri Bendel, Bergdorf Goodman

MAINSTREAM STORE Urban Outfitters and Zara International, "both great for trendy stuff."

FASHION ERA Early '60s

FASHION ICON Jackie O., Grace Kelly, Audrey Hepburn

COLOR TO WEAR Camel

CIRCLE SKIRT

"Sabrina style, with great detailing."

ORT WOOL JACKET

"An unusual color for me, but that's why I bought it—to break up the neutrals in my wardrobe."

BLUE CULT JEANS

"Sexy because they have a little stretch."

"Impractical because they're too high for me, but I love hem—especially the cheetah on he inside that only I can see."

DOLCE & GABBANA LIZARD HEELS

CHAPTER 6

JEANS

VINTAGE

CAPRI

FLARE LEG

STRAIGHT-LEG

BOOTCUT

WIDE-LEG

BOYISH

WHITE

CORDS

fit and styling tips

1 DARK WASH OR FADED?

Dark jeans are cool and classic; they always look right. To keep denim dark, wash inside-out in cold water. If you prefer faded jeans, think about buying a dark pair and letting them evolve in their own time; natural, gradual fading looks much better than factory-fading. (Think of the blonde highlights you get at the beach compared with those that come from the salon.) If you can hold out, it's worth the wait.

FADED

best bet

DARK WASH

SAND-BLASTED

ANTIQUE

baggy *tapered* *high-waisted*

2 LESS FLATTERING, SO WHY EVEN GO THERE?

Baggy jeans can make you look bigger than you are, because your real shape is totally hidden; tapered jeans exaggerate the difference between the upper and lower leg making thighs look bigger; and high-waist jeans accentuate the difference between waist and hips, creating the illusion of broader hips and a wider butt.

3 THE SECRET DOWNSIDE TO STRETCH JEANS

Jeans with stretch are tempting, because they retain their shape. They work well on a full, curvy butt; but if your butt is sort of flat, they can squish it even flatter, so you're better off with good, old fashioned 100% cotton denim. Or try buying them in a size larger than you normally would.

LONGER JEANS=LONGER LEGS

Wear your jeans on the long side, no matter what you have on your feet. With mid-heel boots, the hem of your jeans should wrinkle across the front of the boot and be about 1/4 inch off the floor in back. In flats, the back of the hem should still just about touch the floor.

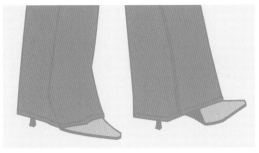

⑤ KEEP YOUR PANTS ON

No one's butt is well-covered in super-low jeans. A belt is key—it truly keeps them on. Be sure to wear low-rise underwear.

⑥ TAKE CARE OF YOUR BEST PAIR

If you have a job that allows for wearing jeans, reserve a pair for work and treat them well. It may sound crazy, but dry-cleaning your work jeans will keep them dark and fresh-looking for a long time.

MAKE YOUR BUTT SMALLER

Little, high pockets make a butt look bigger by tipping the butt-to-pocket ratio the wrong way; so choose larger, centered pockets instead. Back pockets usually look best, but for a pocketless pair, choose jeans with a yoke, which creates a nice curve and breaks up the solid plane of denim.

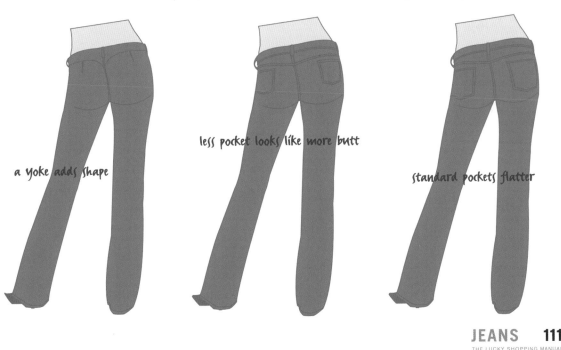

a yoke adds shape

less pocket looks like more butt

standard pockets flatter

jeans that look great on everyone

Flare-leg or bootcut jeans, with a not-too-high rise, happen to be the most flattering, lengthening cut for every body type. It's the *fit* that can make them look particularly amazing on you.

LEG

The ideal pair of bootcut or subtle flare-leg jeans is fitted through the thigh and knee, showing the shape of the leg. Because the flare balances the width of the thigh, the total effect is a long, even shape.

RISE

The crotch-to-waist part of jeans is known as the rise. Choose relatively low-rise jeans that are right for your body. The waist should hit below the belly button, but whether that's one inch or three inches below is up to you. More important is the *fit* of the rise. If fabric bunches up in that area, you might need lower-rise jeans.

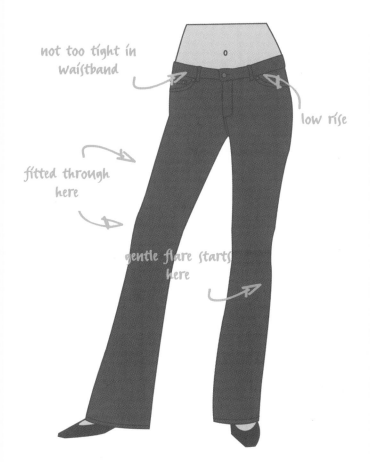

not too tight in waistband

low rise

fitted through here

gentle flare starts here

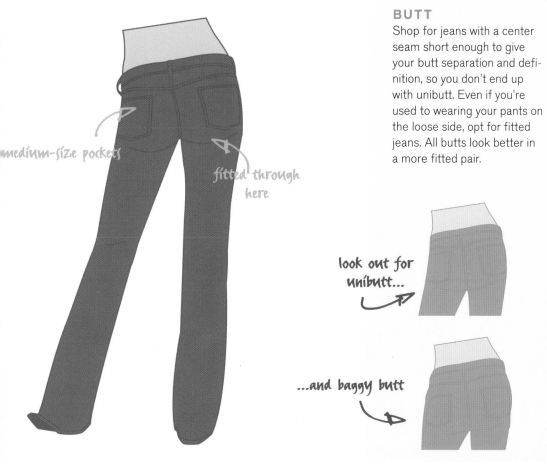

medium-size pockets

fitted through
here

BUTT

Shop for jeans with a center
seam short enough to give
your butt separation and definition, so you don't end up
with unibutt. Even if you're
used to wearing your pants on
the loose side, opt for fitted
jeans. All butts look better in
a more fitted pair.

look out for
unibutt...

...and baggy butt

building a jeans closet

1 PAIR TO WEAR WITH HEELS

1 WEEKEND PAIR YOU CAN WRECK

1 PAIR TO WEAR WITH FLAT

TO WARD OFF LAUNDRY DAY, ADD...

WHITE JEANS

ANOTHER OF YOUR FAVORITE PAIR

CORDS

FUN JEANS

6 ways to wear jeans

CASUAL FRIDAY

WEEKEND

WINTER

BAND-COLLAR COAT
+
LEATHER BAG
+
ANKLE BOOTS

SUMMER

CAMP SHIRT
+
STRAW BAG
+
ESPADRILLES

WINTER

CASHMERE CREWNECK
+
BIG GOLD HOOPS
+
VINTAGE COWBOY BOOTS

SUMMER	WINTER	SUMMER
LACE-TRIM TOP + ETHNIC BELT + ANKLE-TIE THONGS	VELVETEEN JACKET + CHANDELIER EARRINGS + ANKLE BOOTS	SILK SATIN CAMISOLE + CRYSTAL EARRINGS + METALLIC ANKLE-STRAPS

wearing denim with denim

Pairing denims is not a problem. Just keep the washes far
enough apart that it's clear you're not trying to match—or
break up the denim-fest with a bold pattern.

Bright stripes between jacket and jeans can save an outfit from becoming a denim suit, while dark and
light washes in crisp shapes create a nice, clean look.

wear it now, wear it later

SUMMER

White jeans are a sunny backdrop for a classic polo, a bright bucket hat, and casual rainbow slides.

WINTER

With a boatneck, a peacoat, and suede shoe boots, they're part of a crisp, high-contrast winter ensemble.

WHITE JEANS

and you're Rizzo from "Grease"

Too-tight, too-short jeans with heels can look trashy. To mak
this pairing work, choose long bootcut or slightly flared
jeans, and let your legs take credit for how good you look.

OTHER OPTIONS

BOOTCUT

FLARE-LEG

WIDE-LEG

Nice and long

IN THE ● FITTING ROOM

**TRY THE
FRONT POCKETS**

Slide your hands into jeans pockets to check the depth. Front pockets should be pretty shallow; extra fabric here can add bulk.

**CHECK THE
BELT LOOPS**

If you always use a belt, be sure to wear your favorite one when shopping for jeans. Not all belt loops are the same size.

SIT DOWN

If the jeans stand away from your tailbone when you sit or the waistband presses torturously into your lower belly, skip them. Don't buy an uncomfortable pair of jeans—no matter how good they look when you're standing.

**CONSIDER
CUSTOMIZING**

If you find a great-in-the-butt pair of jeans with other fit issues, remember that a few adjustments can turn them into a great-all-over pair. Is the knee too wide? Is there extra fabric in the crotch? Too much bulk in the inner thigh? Identify the problems by pulling the fabric to create the line you want, then go to a tailor with your requests. Your jeans will look great— literally made (over) for you—and you'll wear them forever.

spend or save ?

Don't buy jeans just because of the trendy label. Shop reasonably priced fashion chain stores first, where you can sometimes find designer-esque styling. Jeans are all about the cut and the fit (denim is denim), so if an inexpensive pair looks best, buy them. (If you're very tall and have trouble finding long-enough jeans, you might want to look to designer labels, because they tend to offer more length.) No matter what, stick with cheaper brands for trendy or embellished jeans; if you know you're not going to wear a pair for more than one season, save your money.

KIM FRANCE

JOB:
EDITOR IN CHIEF

STYLE:
DOWNTOWN CLASSIC

"SOMEBODY ONCE said that we're all victims of the era when we first developed our sense of style. That's definitely true for me. My formative period was the early '80s, when I started college; I was just outgrowing Joni Mitchell and discovering the English Beat, and my closet followed along.

"As a freshman, I remember being completely impressed by this particular crowd of older girls from New York and their neat, clean-lined New Wave style. Their look was spare and precise: little cardigans, capri and Keds, in nothing but black and white. Everyone els was still doing the hippie, batik-print thing, and this wa the complete opposite. I was so inspired, I went throug one winter wearing only red and black (red-and-black checked coat; red-and-black striped scarf; a red Betse Johnson sweater with black handprints—you get the picture). I got over the red thing, but the affinity for clean lines and simple shapes stayed with me."

editor of *Lucky*, I hang out with the fashion-department
s most of the day, but I also go to serious meetings
h business types. So my work wardrobe is a mixture of
groovy stuff I'm drawn to and the authoritative touches
job calls for.

little jacket often bridges the gap; it's that one
own-up piece that keeps me prepared for anything. (A
le jacket also makes it possible for me to wear jeans
work, which I do, at least once a week.) I still get to
ar the cool designers I love and make my statement
h a retro print or a touch of lace, but when I need to
ok professional, I do.

took me a while to figure out my formula. I'd made a
ef attempt to handle the fashion overload of this job
th a 'uniform' (a hip suit and white button-down), but
at was quickly abandoned, because it just wasn't me."

CONFIDENCE=STYLE

ven though I nixed the uniform plan, I gravitate toward
apes that flatter me—which is so much more uplifting
an doing the opposite: For a while, I longed to be a pen-
skirt—wearer. It fit my aesthetic—clean, sexy, and cool—
t did nothing for my body. An A-line is my skirt shape, I
w know beyond a shadow of a doubt. Along with fabu-
us jackets and A-lines, my work staples include pretty,
ted tops; jeans; slouchy black trousers; and great boots.

ll winter long I wear black boots with skirts and black
hts; I've never subscribed to the bare-knee look in the
eezing cold, and although this puts me in the distinct
nority among female editors in chief, I'll stick with what
akes me comfortable.

o me, that's a big part of being stylish: looking comfort-
le and projecting confidence. It's about ease. You'll see it
the models we cast in *Lucky*, and you'll see it if you
roll around our offices: More than any piece of clothing or
ir of shoes, style is simply about feeling good."

from kim's closet

LACE TOP

"A vintagey little top under a jacket keeps my work look from being too business-y."

"I picked this up on a business trip to Milan. It stays crisp on the hottest, limpest, most soul-depleting summer days."

PRADA SKIRT

RUFFLE TOP

"I saw this in L.A. one day, bu passed it up. It haunted me, an everyone at Lucky felt my pain. week later Andrea bought it for as a surprise—and, independent' so did the fashion department Yes, now I have two!"

MY FAVORITES:

DESIGNER "Do you have an hour?"

SHOES "Everything from Timberland boots to Louboutin pumps."

JEANS "I have every trendy brand in my closet, but Levi's remain the gold standard."

HIGH-END STORES Kirna Zabete, in Manhattan; Fred Segal, in L.A.

MAINSTREAM STORES Gap, Club Monaco, DKNY

FASHION ERA The '60s. "So much was going on, from moddishness to hippie-dom."

FASHION ICON "I've never had an icon but would love to possess Faye Dunaway's wardrobe from *Network*."

COLORS TO WEAR Black, white, navy, and occasionally red or pink

"A gift from a friend that I love"

LUCKY LOCKET

"These shoes are a few seasons old, and I love them. Whenever I have a lunch at the Four Seasons, I find myself choosing them. It's nice to stand out in the sea of Manolos."

"I don't know if I've ever looked chicer than I did when m mother dressed me. Sometime when I'm stuck on what to we I wish my mom would come p together my outfit."

CHUNKY MARYJANES

ROCK-CHICK BAG

"No matter what I have on, I always look 80% cooler if I'm carrying this bag."

CHANEL WATCH

"There's something super-chic about the black face of this perfect watch."

CHLOÉ
VELVET GOWN

"So sexy and feminine without being at all flouncy. One of those really special pieces that makes me feel great the minute I put it on."

"When I bought this on sale in 1996 (a big purchase for me then), I never imagined it would have such staying power. I still break it out every winter."

HELMUT LANG PEACOAT

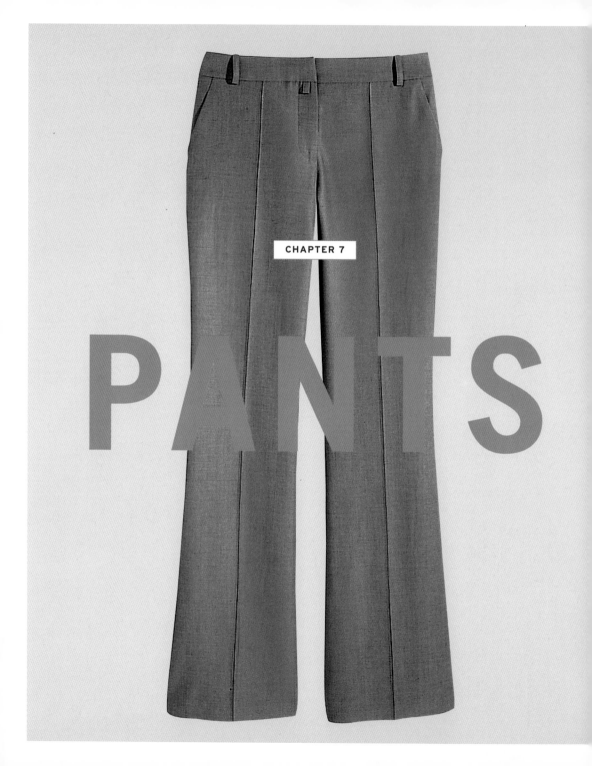

CHAPTER 7

PANTS

CARGO

WIDE-LEG

CHINOS

CIGARETTE

CUFFED

SAILOR

CROPPED

EVENING

PINSTRIPE

fit and styling tips

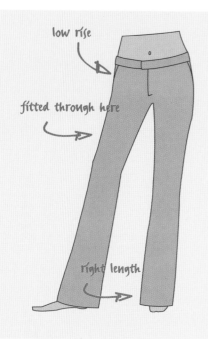

low rise

fitted through here

right length

① PERFECT FIT

The fit of pants varies according to style, but most work best in a low-rise cut that's tailored through the hips and butt. Dressy evening pants should be slightly sexier than daytime pants. Wear all styles long (except cigarette pants, which have to end at the ankle); it's a classic flattering line. Hem pants to hit right at the bottom of the heel.

② CASUAL DOESN'T HAVE TO MEAN SCHLUMPY

Weekend pants shouldn't look sloppy. Mak an effort to find flattering shapes in casua styles, and have them hemmed to the prop length. In chinos, a low rise and a slight fla leg looks good on everyone. Watch out for slash pockets, though, which can make hip look bigger. Save extremely casual pants— like drawstrings—for bed and the gym.

look for weekend pants that flatte

too loose

correct fit

Pants look good with heels, but some styles just don't work on a practical level. Don't wear heels with wide-leg cuffed pants, because your heel can easily get caught in these. Wear flats or wedges instead. Skip ankle straps with cropped pants, because this combo cuts the legs twice, and makes them look shorter.

FITTING WIDE-LEG PANTS

These can look good on almost everyone, but watch the fit; they have to be snug in the hips and waist, to show your shape, then gently widen. A loose fit up top can make you look stocky instead of long and lean.

WHAT THE TAILOR CAN FIX

A tailor can take in the waist of a pair of pants, if needed, and can alter the shape of the leg, for a more flattering line. If the crotch of the pants is hanging a little low, alterations will help there, too. Pants that come with cuffs should keep them when hemmed, because that's part of the design, but don't create cuffs where there are none.

6 TROUSERS NEVER FAIL

Throw on a pair of menswear trousers in the morning, and you'll feel confident for the rest of the day. They're both authoritative and graceful, flattering and comfortable. Perfect for the office, they can also be dressed up for evening with a sexy, fun little top and heels.

7 THE BEST FABRICS

Work pants in lightweight wool or a comparable blend always look good; the tiniest percentage of stretch in the fabric helps their shape. Watch out for narrow, fitted shapes in stretch cotton, though; cotton pants with too much stretch can hike up your leg.

pants that look great on everyone

Menswear-style pants have a Katharine Hepburn elegance and are kind to all figures.

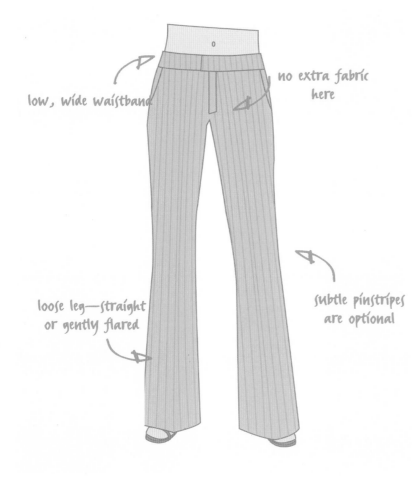

low, wide waistband

no extra fabric here

loose leg—straight or gently flared

subtle pinstripes are optional

FRONT
Look for a dark-neutral pair with a slim fit through the hips that gives way to fuller legs. A comfortable, low rise with a wider-than-usual waistband is particularly flattering. While legs are loose, they shouldn't be shapeless. Trousers that show the outline of your upper leg and flare from the knee down add length; a small amount of stretch in the fabric can help.

BACK

Regarding the rear view, as with jeans, pocket placement is everything. Small, straight slash pockets that fall a little higher than mid-butt are most flattering. Although they're full in the legs, menswear trousers should fit well through the seat; the crotch should have no more than a half inch of fabric hanging.

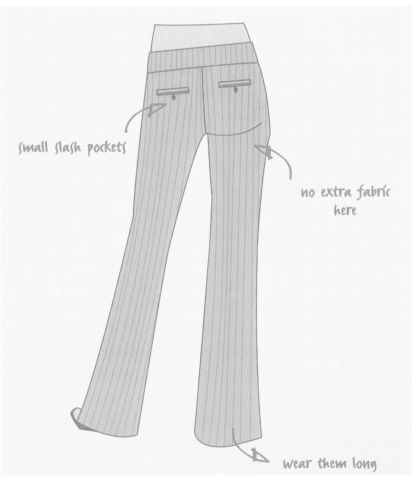

small slash pockets

no extra fabric here

wear them long

the best pants for you

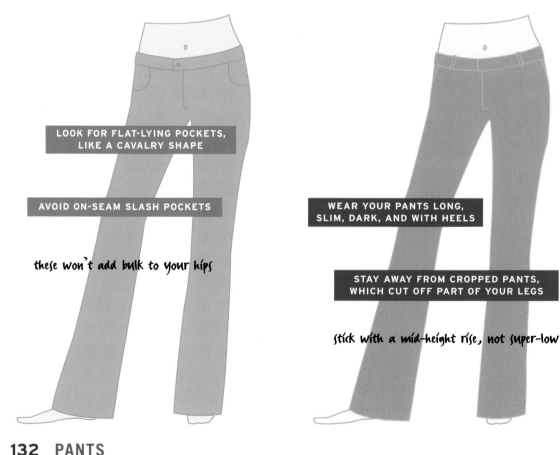

IF YOU'RE PEAR-SHAPED...

LOOK FOR FLAT-LYING POCKETS, LIKE A CAVALRY SHAPE

AVOID ON-SEAM SLASH POCKETS

these won't add bulk to your hips

IF YOU HAVE SHORT LEGS...

WEAR YOUR PANTS LONG, SLIM, DARK, AND WITH HEELS

STAY AWAY FROM CROPPED PANTS, WHICH CUT OFF PART OF YOUR LEGS

stick with a mid-height rise, not super-low

IF YOU HAVE BIG THIGHS...

IF YOU'RE STRAIGHT AND NARROW TRY...

BOYISH PANTS

CROPPED PANTS

WEAR SLIGHTLY WIDE-LEG PANTS
THAT ARE FITTED THROUGH THE HIPS

AVOID TAPERED PANTS, WHICH EXAGGERATE
THE DIFFERENCE BETWEEN THIGHS AND CALVES

CIGARETTE PANTS

building a pants closet

3 PAIRS OF WINTER WORK PANTS

tropical wool, or a comparable blend

3 PAIRS OF SUMMER WORK PANTS

2 PAIRS OF
ALL-SEASON
WEEKEND PANTS

satin, for winter and summer

1 PAIR OF
LIGHTWEIGHT
EVENING PANTS

building a pants closet

MORE WINTER WORK PANTS

A PAIR OF FUN PANTS

VELVET OR SATIN EVENING PANTS

MORE SUMMER WORK PANTS

wear it now, wear it later

WINTER

With ribbon-wrapped pumps and a not-so-fancy drapey tee, satin evening pants are just right for dinner out.

SUMMER

Pair them with a vivid silk camisole and metallic sandals for an all-out dressy look in summer.

ATIN EVENING PANTS

3 pants, 2 ways

TUXEDO PANTS

CARG

DAY

T-SHIRT
+
FLOWER-STUD EARRINGS
+
ATHLETIC SHOES

EVENING

FLUTTER-SLEEVE TOP
+
GOLD EARRINGS
+
EMBELLISHED SANDALS

DAY

RIBBED TANK
+
STRAW BAG
+
PINK SNEAKERS

a party look for someone who's not into dressing up

MENSWEAR TROUSERS

EVENING

SILK HALTER
+
BEADED PURSE
+
METALLIC SANDALS

DAY

SILK BLOUSE
+
DIAMOND STUDS
+
SPECTATOR PUMPS

EVENING

SEQUIN TOP
+
DANGLY EARRINGS
+
HIGH-HEEL THONGS

*ghttime
k with
e charm*

CROPPED PANTS

With a crisp wrap shirt and stiletto boots, cropped weekend pants take on a whole new vibe. A jacket and D'Orsay pumps also render them office-worthy.

Wearing casual pants to work is easy, if you top them with something structured but not overly dressy. Subtly step up the look another notch with elegant footwear.

CHINOS

Chinos look right at home with a rich wool blazer and red tassel pumps. A feminine cotton shirt and perforated slingbacks work because they're professional but not stuffy.

and you've got a bad case of grandpa-butt

Achieving a slouchy effect in menswear pants means walking a fine line. Loose legs look graceful, but a low-hanging crotch does not. Stick with a slim fit through the hips and seat, with some stretch in the fabric.

OTHER OPTIONS

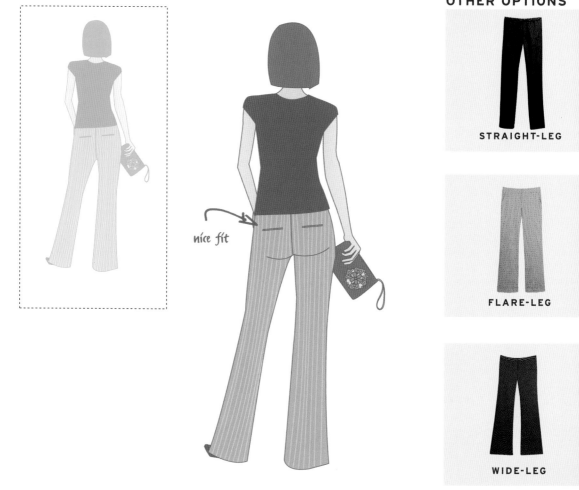

nice fit

STRAIGHT-LEG

FLARE-LEG

WIDE-LEG

IN THE ● FITTING ROOM

WEAR THE RIGHT SHOES

If you know what type of pants you're shopping for, wear (or bring) shoes that will go with them. Heels, for example, will make a big difference in how evening pants or work pants will look.

TAKE A WALK

Tapered pants (like side-zip cigarette pants) with stretch can sometimes inch up your leg little by little as you move. Test-walk them to see if they need constant tugging down. Check the front of any pair of pants after a walk; if you see a "smiley face" (horizontal wrinkles) emanating from the crotch, they're not a great fit.

HAVE A SEAT

When you sit down and your thighs spread a little, tailored pants—especially those that are very fitted through the upper leg—can suddenly be surprisingly tight. Try gently sliding up the fabric in the thigh before you sit, to see if that helps. If not, choose another style.

LISTEN TO YOUR LEGS

Some unlined wool pants can be itchy; it's one of those things that's easy to ignore in the fitting room but makes itself apparent upon first wearing. To test a pair with itch potential, keep them on for a while in the store as you revisit the racks or try on tops.

spend or save ?

Spend on menswear trousers, where fit counts most, and the quality of the fabric affects the way the pants fall. You'll wear them into the ground, so they're worth the investment. Save on chinos, cargo pants, and other weekend wear; you don't want to have to take special care of them. It's better to buy cheap, let them fade or stain, and replace them when you need to.

CHAPTER 8

SUITS

CLASSIC SKIRT SUIT

GIRLY SKIRT SUIT

EVENING SKIRT SUIT

BOYISH SUIT

CLASSIC PANTS SUIT

EVENING SUIT

fit and styling tips

1 PERFECT FIT

A suit is meant to look sharp, so steer clear of soft-edged ensembles posing as suits: The vibe you're going for is clean and crisp. Your jacket should fit well through the shoulder and under-arm. When closed, it should lie flat, with no pulling across the chest or around the buttons. Pants should be fitted through the hip, but should never be very tight. The sleeve of the jacket should end at the heel of your hand; err on the side of too long, if there's any question.

wear your collar in or out

2 WHICH BUTTONS TO CLOSE

Wear your suit jacket with the top button (or the top two buttons) closed, not only the bottom button closed. If you ever have occasion to wear a double-breasted suit, keep in mind that the jacket is designed to be worn completely closed.

3 SHIRT COLLAR OPTIONS

If you wear a button-down shirt with a suit, you ha[ve] the collar-placement dilemma to deal with—but there's no wrong answer here. Outside your jacke[t] lapel is a little downtown; inside has a kind of soph[is]ticated French feel.

4 KEY WORD: PROPORTION

Look at a suit as a whole piece, rather than as a jacket and pants; the shape should work overall, a[nd] none of the elements should be exaggerated. If th[e] jacket is cut long, then the pants should be longis[h] too. A cropped jacket makes sense with slim, tailo[red] trousers that are mid- to high-waisted, because a low-waisted pair would reveal the shirt between th[e] pants and jacket.

KNOW YOUR OPTIONS

A visual glossary to help you navigate the sometimes intimidating world of suits.

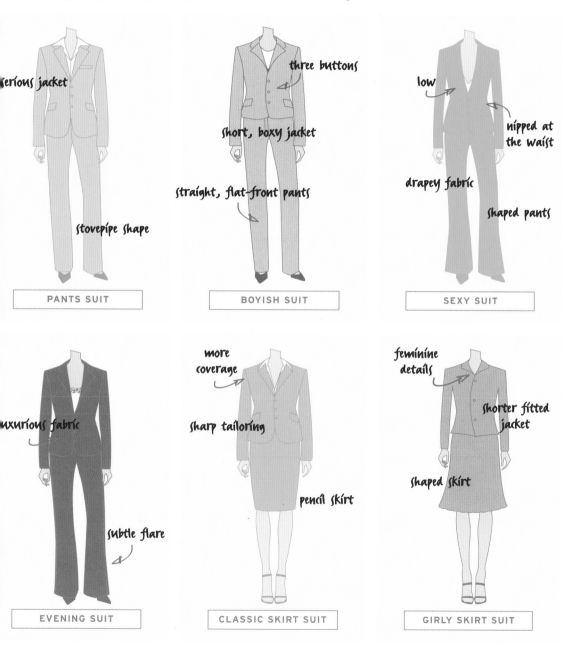

serious jacket

three buttons

short, boxy jacket

straight, flat-front pants

stovepipe shape

PANTS SUIT

BOYISH SUIT

low

nipped at the waist

drapey fabric

shaped pants

SEXY SUIT

luxurious fabric

subtle flare

EVENING SUIT

more coverage

sharp tailoring

pencil skirt

CLASSIC SKIRT SUIT

feminine details

shorter fitted jacket

shaped skirt

GIRLY SKIRT SUIT

the best suits for you

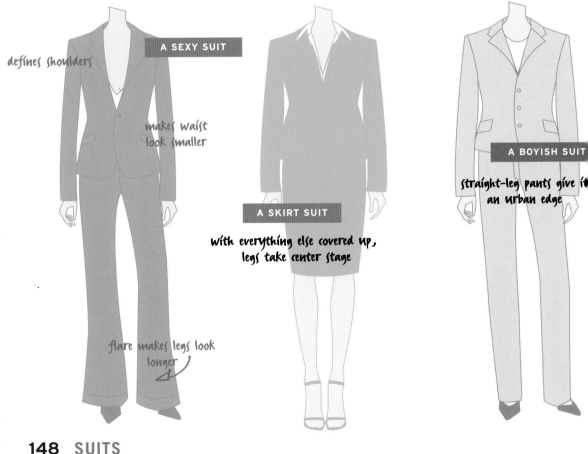

defines shoulders

A SEXY SUIT

makes waist look smaller

flare makes legs look longer

A SKIRT SUIT

with everything else covered up, legs take center stage

A BOYISH SUIT

straight-leg pants give it an urban edge

making a plain suit sexy

Show a hint of lace or satin peeking out of your suit jacket for a sexy, sophisticated evening look. But choose a top that's not too lingerie-ish; you want to be able to lose the jacket and still look put-together when the dance floor heats up.

building a suit closet

2 CLASSIC SUITS

serious for work, but versatile

1 SKIRT SUIT

a trendy shape for work or nighttime

IF YOU ADORE SUITS, ADD...

TWO FUN SUITS

another evening suit

(1) **EVENING SUIT**

you'll wear the pants all the time

3 suits, 2 ways

BOYISH SUIT

SKIR

SERIOUS	FUN	SERIOUS
CRISP SHIRT + **GOLD BRACELET** + **POINTY PUMPS**	**LACY TOP** + **WESTERN BELT** + **ANKLE BOOTS**	**HIGHNECK BLOUS** + **KNOT BRACELET** + **KITTEN-HEEL SLINGB**

FUN

HALTER TOP
+
EMBROIDERED BAG
+
ANKLE-STRAP HEELS

SERIOUS

KNIT TOP
+
LOGO WATCH
+
SLEEK SANDALS

FUN

RIBBON-TRIM TOP
+
SILVER DROP EARRINGS
+
ANKLE-TIE HEELS

ONE FALSE MOVE...
and it's Victor Victoria

A classic pants suit is inherently masculine, but a stiff button-down can push it in the wrong direction. For evening use the neckline as a zone of femininity. Just stick with the basics: silk, lace, and a little cleavage.

OTHER OPTIONS

TIE-BACK LACE

PLUNGING NECKLINE

ASYMMETRIC HEM

IN THE FITTING ROOM

SHOP TOPS

Find two appropriate tops in the store to try on with a suit; don't make such a major decision based on how a suit looks with the tee you wore shopping that day.

CONSIDER THE FABRIC

A nice, light material can be used year-round, so keep your eye on tropical wool and microfibers. Avoid heavy wool suits; though cool and retro-looking, they're uncomfortable worn indoors, even in the dead of winter, and are frequently less than slimming. In the summer months, consider a nice cotton or seersucker suit.

LOOK AT THE DETAILS

Stay away from heavy-handed, trendy extras, like lace-up sides on the jacket. But hunt down subtle, sophisticated, classic details like pintucking, which can step up a suit and make it special.

spend or save ?

Don't try to save money on a suit. It's an important part of your wardrobe, and you want to be able to wear it for years. Buy the best quality suit you can afford—especially when it comes to classic styles. If you need a shot of justification, think of all the wear you'll get out of it as separates.

LUCKY GIRL

shoshanna lonstein

JOB:
CLOTHING DESIGNER

STYLE:
SIMPLE AND SEXY

HER RULES...

1 "Wear only shapes that complement your body, regardless of
trends; if you look great, that's a
anyone's going to notice."

2 "If you have sexy features, tame
your clothing; the contrast work:

3 "Style means walking confidently
and knowing you look good—not
tugging at your dress or hiding
your bra straps."

FAMOUSLY CURVY Shoshanna Lonstein says her desire to design was fueled by complex feelings about clothes. "My love-hate relationship with fashion inspired me. I was not an ideal 2, 4, or 6, so I was limited as to the clothing I could wear and feel great in. I was small, but my proportion was not." Lonstein succeeded because she saw a gap in the market, and filled it with elegant, feminine pieces that flatter all body types, but especially meet the needs of curvy women. "Unlike some people who design for a character," says Shoshanna, "I only design clothes I can wear."

Her pretty, tailored line of clothing is a huge success, and it all grew out of her personal style. "I would never hide my body," she says. "I don't wear oversize things."

For daytime, Shoshanna's drawn to menswear pieces: "Very feminine bodies look sexy in men's clothing. I love the look of a fitted button-down with jeans and boots." And nighttime is all about her own designs: "I like my arms and shoulders and collarbones, so I often wear strapless tops—a straight-across bustline and a fitted waist."

"I look to the past, the '40s, '50s, and '60s, for ideas— times that celebrated women's bodies." As a result Shoshanna's designs have a retro look, but that's accidental. "They're classic shapes and my clothes are classic clothes—sexy but not overtly sexy."

"I'm proud of my body but I won't wear something down to my belly button. A woman with a feminine shape knows she doesn't have to call attention to it; it does that all by itself."

closet

from shoshanna's

"Pearls and a sexy dress are a great juxtaposition. For a dressy event, I might wear these with the pretty clasp in front."

PEARLS

"I love designing feminine necklines that leave room for jewelry."

TORTOISE VINTAGE BAG

"I got this at the Portobello Market in London. It's fun to imagine where it's been and who used to carry it."

SHOSHANNA EYELE[T] TOP AND SKIRT

SHOSHANNA CASHMERE SWEATER

"My whole showroom is mint green. This sweater looks great against tanned skin and with denim."

MY FAVORITES:

DESIGNER Badgley Mischka

SHOES "I'm madly in love with all my shoes. I can't insult any of them by picking just one pair."

JEANS Levi's 501s. "I've been wearing them since seventh grade."

HIGH-END STORES Fred Segal and Bergdorf Goodman

MAINSTREAM STORE Abercrombie & Fitch

FASHION ERA The '50s. "It was so glamorous—people dressed up and did their hair every day. It was a happy time, and it showed in the clothes."

FASHION ICON Sophia Loren

COLORS TO WEAR Mint green, lavender, pink, and light blue

PRADA MULES

"I love little details that make a shoe special."

OLD VINTAGE BAG

"My mother is a huge antiques collector, and she got me into collecting vintage handbags. I'll wear them to black-tie events, but otherwise I'm careful with them—I keep them in bubble wrap at home."

HAIR CLIP

"I bought this from a street vendor in New York—almost looks like jewelry."

"I love bright colors with my hair and olive skin. For work, I might throw this on with a floral-print cotton skirt."

CASHMERE SHELL

CMAN WATCH

"I rarely wear bracelets, but I have a few watches that can dress up jeans or—like this one—almost go black tie."

CHAPTER 9

BAGS

CLUTCH

DRAWSTRING

LADY

HOBO

STRAW

FRAMED

BEACH

SADDLE

CRESCENT

TOTE

BRIEFCASE

FRINGE

LOGO

MESSENGER

ROUND-HANDLE

SHOULDER

shopping and styling tips

① PAY ATTENTION TO YOUR BAG

Just as a nice, well-maintained bag can make you look put together, one that's messed-up can throw your whole look off. Your bag is part of your outfit, so keep it clean and take it to a shoemaker if it needs repairs. A good bag should last years, style-wise—so do your best to take care of it.

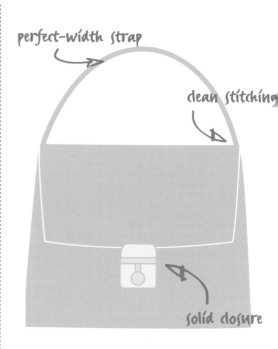

perfect-width strap

clean stitching

solid closure

② EVEN IN THE HEADY WORLD OF BAGS, BE PRACTICAL

Apply logic when bag shopping: Don't get a huge tote with a skinny strap, because it will cut into your shoulder and be hard to carry. Don't buy a short-handle bag to wear with a bulky coat; it won't stay up. Your everyday bag and your work bag need to be easy to use, so skip those with complicated closures; opt for magnetic snaps underneath buckles if you can find them.

③ WHAT TO LOOK FOR IN AN EXPENSIVE BAG

A well-made bag is truly one of life's greatest joys, so make sure you're getting what you've paid for. Watch for solid-feeling and sound-functioning hardware; pockets that open and close cleanly and lie as they should; an appropriate length and width strap (or an adjustable one); and secure, even stitching.

⑤ THE BAGS-AND-SHOES QUESTION

You wouldn't wear wallabees with a lady bag, but it's also not a good idea to put fringe boots with a fringe bag. Don't worry about clashing or mixing materials. Just think about keeping the level of dressiness somewhat in line—casual shoes with a casual bag, and vice versa. Beyond that, be loose. If it looks fine to you, it probably is.

---

⑥ ARE YOU THE HANDBAG TYPE?

A small, short-strapped purse is undoubtedly elegant. But carrying one regularly requires a certain personality (organized), along with an ability to travel light. Don't fall for the hot handbag of the season if you always carry way too much stuff for it to hold. It'll end up sitting on a shelf in your closet.

④ HANDLING THE BOTTOMLESS-PIT BAG

It's impossible to look cool while madly rummaging through the contents of a big tote in search of a tiny sunken item. An oversize bag needs to have easy access compartments on the outside and inside to hold all the necessities: wallet, mobile phone, keys, lipstick, and sunglasses, at the very least. Think before you are seduced by the chic lines of an impractical, big, pocketless bag.

THE LUCKY SHOPPING MANUAL

shopping and styling tips

coat bunches up   looks right

8 LUG YOUR GEAR AND STILL LOOK PROFESSIONAL

If you always carry a ton of stuff to work, use a big tote with shoulder straps, and tuck a cute little handbag inside. Take just the small bag to lunches and meetings, so you don't feel like a pack animal all the time.

9 COMFORTABLE CLUTCH

Make sure that any clutch you buy has a little wrist strap. Without a strap, even something as simple as having a drink becomes an effort, because your clutch is always occupying one of your hands.

7 PICK THE COAT FOR THE BAG OR THE BAG FOR THE COAT?

Your bag needs to function well with a range of coats and jackets. Don't worry about every piece of outerwear you have, but keep your big-ticket items in synch (overcoat and everyday bag; overcoat and work tote), and think about both form and function: A cross-strap bag, for example, doesn't work with the clean lines of a lady coat; a handbag makes more sense.

IS A STATUS BAG WORTH IT?

If you don't mind spending the money, an obviously designer bag gives you a certain cachet. Like pricey jewelry, it's a fashion statement all on its own that lets you look cool even when you're not so put together. But if you're going to invest in a designer bag, be sure not to buy a trendy shape; choose a classic that will pack a punch for many years.

MAKE SURE YOUR BAG GOES WITH YOUR SIZE

If you're a big woman, a very small bag is not a great idea; it's more flattering to carry a larger style. Funny enough, the reverse doesn't always hold true: A little woman can look cool even with a big bag.

12 WEARING A LONG-STRAP BAG

Casual long-strap bags, aka saddle bags, look great worn across the body over a jacket or sweater. But with a T-shirt, where the strap would cut in a cross-your-heart-bra way, let the bag hang off one shoulder instead. Find a saddle bag with an adjustable strap, so you have options and can customize for height; if you're on the short side, a too-long bag will bang against your thigh with every step you take.

building a bags closet

1 EVERYDAY BAG

stick with black or dark brown

1 SMALL WORK BAG

1 WORK TOTE O BRIEF- CASE

whichever is right for your job

1 EVENING BAG

1 CASUAL TOTE

inexpensive and washable—for the supermarket, the beach, the gym

1 SMALL GOING-OU BAG

just big enough for your wa keys, and lipstick

IF MONEY IS NO OBJECT, ADD...

A SUMMER EVENING BAG

SOME FUN GOING-OUT BAGS

A STRAW TOTE

in a light-colored fabric or leather

A SUMMER WORK BAG

A WINTER EVENING BAG

for hands-free shopping

A LONG-STRAP BAG

holds all your inflight gear

A GIANT TOTE FOR TRAVEL

be sure it stands up on its own

A WATERPROOF BEACH BAG

pick your favorites

PURSE

HANDBAG

HOBO

PATCHWORK

QUILTED

FRINGE-ZIP

PATTERNED

BELTED

SNAP-FRONT

HARNESS

SUEDE

RETRO

pick your favorites

LEATHER SHOPPER

BUCKET BAG

FLAP BAG

CALFSKIN BUCKLE BAG

LEATHER-TRIMMED CANVAS

SQUARE TOTE

SILK-AND-MESH DRAWSTRING

METAL MESH

SEQUIN PURSE

LOGO CLUTCH

GATHERED METALLIC

SEQUIN ROUND-HANDLE

bags and outerwear

TOGGLE COAT
+
LEATHER-TRIMMED DENIM BAG

LADY COAT
+
LADY BAG

BLACK OVERCOAT
+
BROWN SHOULDER BAG

black meets brown in a rich combo

casual and clean

perfect—
a heavier bag wouldn't look right

SHEARLING COAT
+
DISTRESSED HIPPIE BAG

TRENCH COAT
+
CONTRAST LEATHER TOTE

PARKA
+
LOGO CARRYALL

both bag and coat are groovy and relaxed

red piping brightens a serious trench

the parka is made cool by association

change your bag, change your look

A SKIRT SUIT CAN BE...

DENI

CORPORATE

VINTAGEY

With a trendy skirt suit, a leather briefcase means business. Switch to a vintage lady bag, and you suddenly have a retro edge.

A WHITE TEE CAN BE...

A WHITE TEE CAN BE...

PREPPY

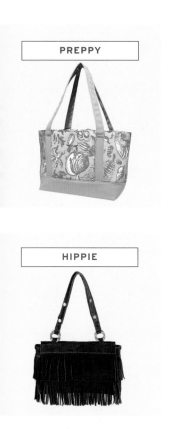

HIPPIE

Weekend jeans with a playful pink-and-green bag says cool prepster. Switch to an oversize fringe bag, and you've wandered to the hackeysack-playing part of the quad.

FUNKY

POLISHED

With a plaid monster bag, a simple tee and black pants are totally downtown. Switch to a sharp structured tote, and the look is more Fifth Avenue.

wear it now, wear it later

WINTER

Against a neat jacket-and-jeans ensemble, i
works with a bright patchwork scarf to loose
sharp lines and shake up a winter palette.

SUMMER

**WHITE LEATHER
BAG**

+

This structured shoulder bag is part of an ed
day-to-night look with a filmy tunic, a pencil
skirt and delicate ankle straps.

breaking bag boundaries

Add a little whimsy to an outfit with an unexpected bag. Just be sure to keep all your other pieces in line and let the bag be the single contradiction.

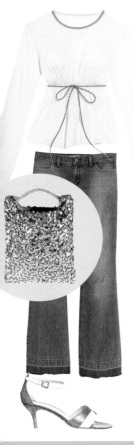

sequin evening bag gives eans and a velvet-trimmed op an eclectic sophistication.

Paired with a corduroy blazer, menswear pants, and pumps, a backpack becomes office-worthy.

A sophisticated weekend look gets earthy with a big straw bag.

and fee-fi-fo-fum

A big coat and a little bag give you a land-of-the-giants vibe. Balance the bulk of a parka with a more substantial messenger-style bag that hangs comfortably across your body.

OTHER OPTIONS

the bag falls short

makes more sense

SLEEK

WEATHERED

UTILITARIAN

AT THE BAG STORE

WEAR THE RIGHT CLOTHES

When shopping, try to wear the coat you'll typically use with your bag. If you're looking for a bag you'll use in summer, try it with a tank, to be sure the its comfortable against bare skin. Some summer materials—like straw and raw-edged natural leather—can be harsh.

FILL IT UP

Empty totes stuffed with paper usually sit nicely on the shoulder. Full bags can press uncomfortably, or lose their shape. When checking out large bags, drop your own bag inside to get a sense of what the bag looks and feels like in action.

TROUBLE-SHOOT

It's depressing to buy a bag only to later discover it can't, for example, stand up without tipping over on a restroom vanity. So reality-test a bag in the store by walking with it squished under your arm; undoing the closures one-handed (and quickly); and dropping it on the floor, the way you will after you've owned it for a week.

spend or save?

Spend on your big work bag and your everyday bag; both should be durable, great-looking, and truly functional. A classic bag you know you'll use forever—like a good black leather bag—is also worth the money. Save on trendy going-out bags or summer bags, which get lots of wear and tear.

ANDREA LINETT

JOB:
CREATIVE DIRECTOR

STYLE:
UNTUCKED GLAMOUR

"WHEN I WAS LITTLE, my mom was really groovy. She used to get her hair cut on St. Mark Place, at Paul MacGregor (he did the *Klute* haircut fo Jane Fonda). I'd sit on the floor and watch everyone, just taking it all in—their shoes, their belts, the cut of their jeans. It was so exciting. I must have been about five at the time. But I'm not all that different now; I sti get really excited when I see people with great style. I know it sounds like a cliché, but I don't like fashion. I' much more into people and how they put things together; I'd rather see the models backstage in their own clothes than watch them on the runway."

ON STYLE
"Style to me is people who always look like themselves, matter what—and who don't look like they're trying. I thi it's about finding what works for you and sticking with it and not following what other people do. It's not necessa about wearing a uniform, but definitely having an identifia

k. When people see something and say, 'Oh, that's so
,' it means you have a style all your own."

TRENDS

on't care what celebrities or editors are wearing.
ually I'm turned off by things when everybody has
m. I'm not into trends for their own sake, but some-
es I'll make one up for myself."

TAKING CONTROL

a customizer. I'll buy dresses and chop them off, or
a brooch to change a neckline so it shows off my
ulders better. I've cut off parts of shoes. If something
esn't look right, I try to figure out how to make it work
me and fix it."

EVERYDAY CLOTHES

ear jeans 98% of the time. For tops, I like sexy styles
t drape, in neutral colors, but nothing too frilly—it
ays has to have a bit of an edge. And I'll usually have
nething I can add on top that keeps me from looking
a slob—a cool sweater or jacket. Almost everything I
ar comes from Martin, my friend Anne Johnston
ert's line and store, plus I have a lot of vintage stuff."

DETAILS

lways wear belts—for the old-fashioned reason of
ding up my pants, as well as for style. And I'm
sessed with jewelry. I have a huge collection—every-
ng from a gold nameplate to handmade silver stuff to
paste to punk."

DRESSING UP

not a dressy person. I always feel really ugly when
making such an effort to look pretty; I'm much hap-
r being myself. So if I need to dress up, I usually
lude something that's dressed down too—like clunky
es with a fancy, ethereal dress. I used to worry
ut what's appropriate, but I don't care anymore—I
t wear what's appropriate for me."

"Has actual flecks of metal woven in, and makes any outfit rock-n-roll elegant."

SILVER BELT BUCKLE

GAUZE SEQUIN SCARF

"From my belt-buckle collection. 1965 is the year I was born."

"A never-worn vintage piec[e] that fits so well. I bought i[t] in brown, too."

MY FAVORITES:

DESIGNER "I don't really have a lot of designer clothes, except vintage-designer. I do like Rick Owens and Anne Johnston Albert, because their stuff is sexy and easy to wear."

SHOES "For some reason, I always feel most confident in boots."

JEANS Martin and Levi's

HIGH-END STORES "Barneys New York and Maxfield's in L.A. to get ideas, but I usually buy in vintage stores, like Amarcord (N.Y.), Foley + Corrina (N.Y.), and Wasteland (L.A.)."

FASHION ERA Late '60s/early '70s. "the glamrock—David Bowie era"

STYLE ICONS Marianne Faithfull, Jane Birkin and Bianca Jagger, in the '60s and '70s. Kate Moss, now. "Sexy, bohemian women who make it look easy."

MOTORCYCLE JACKET

HERMÈS WATCH

"The middle ope[ns] it's the perfect ma[rriage] of high-end glam[our] and rock-chick co[ol]"

GOLD CLOGS
"Comfortable and glamorous."

**DIAMOND AND
JADE BIRD GOLD RING**

" A totally crazy ring,
from a pawn shop
in Tucson."

ARMY FUR COAT

" My idea of a fancy coat:
a custom-made fur lining
for my army jacket."

"My mom's, from
the '60s. I love how
sexy it is."

WESTERN BELT

"A real rodeo belt, bearing my
first and middle name—
a gift from friends."

**VINTAGE
LEATHER BAG**

DANGLY INDIAN EARRINGS

" I wore these virtually
every day one winter."

COWBOY BOOTS

" I like the deep color of
22-karat gold best."

CHAPTER 10

SHOES

STRAPPY

ANKLE STRAP

PLATFORM

CUT-OUT

STILETTO

THONG

FLAT

TWO-TONE

ANKLE BOOT

WEDGE

T-STRAP

LOAFER

CLOG

D'ORSAY

MULE

METALLIC

KNEE BOOT

ROUND TOE

EMBELLISHED

COWBOY BOOT

KITTEN HEEL

FLIP FLOP

SLIDE

fit and styling tips

boots are too loose   just right fit

② STYLE VS. COMFORT

Suffering for the sake of a perfect pair of shoes is misguided, because if your feet are aching, you won't look cool, no matter what you're wearing. Think of how effortlessly you strut in your favorite boots; that's the essence of coolness in footwear—walking with confidence. So skip shoes that hurt or are ill-fitting or awkward. Save very high heels and delicate fabrics for special occasions.

① PERFECT FIT: KNEE BOOTS

Boots should be tapered at the ankle and fit well through the calf. Ideally, they'll hug your leg just under the knee. If most boots you try on are big in the shaft, look for a pair with a buckle at the top so you can adjust them. If a too-tight shaft is always a problem, do a little research online; some fashion chains and catalogs offer boots in additional calf sizes.

③ HOW TO BREAK IN NEW SHOES

Wear new shoes for a little while, then switch—don't wear them for two days in a row. And remember: It's not worth it to wear great new shoes when your feet are covered in bandages.

KEEP YOUR SHOES ON

Be sure that strappy barely-there heels fit snugly; walking in too-big sandals is a real struggle. But if you're between sizes in boots, round up for comfort. There's no chance they'll fall off, and your feet will be warm—and expanding—inside. When shopping for slingbacks, look for a pair with elastic sewn into the back of the strap, which guarantees a more secure fit.

CLASSIC SHOES

In footwear, "classic" goes beyond brown and black leather: snake, alligator, satin, velvet, natural leather, metallic, and leopard are all reliable places to invest your shoe dollars.

HEIGHT WITHOUT HEELS

If you have a hard time wearing skinny heels but you like some extra height, some '40s-style platform heels are a great option. They're much less challenging to walk in. Beware of wedges with a low front, though, which are just as tricky as, if not trickier than, heels.

flip-flops are respectable with a casual summer dress

8 COMFORTABLE, CHEAP, COOL

Flip-flops are totally acceptable with a casual summer slipdress; just be sure they're not dirty or beat up. A classic flip-flop is flat and plain; platform or embellished versions come and go. Whatever style you choose, be sure they're comfy between the toes.

TAKING CARE OF YOUR SHOES

Have the shoemaker put a piece of thin rubber on the bottom of all style shoes for traction and protection. For those shoes or boots you want to be able to wear in all kinds of weather, thicker rubber on the bottom can create an impenetrable waterproof layer. Visit the shoemaker for reheeling and resoling as needed—don't wait for holes or until the heel is worn down to the metal.

shoes that flatter your legs

ALWAYS FLATTERING

HARD TO WEAR

in flats, more skin is better

ALWAYS FLATTERING

HARD TO WEAR

gives the ankle shape

leg blends into foot—in a bad way

BALLET FLATS
with shorter skirts can make calves look short and wide.

FLIP-FLOPS AND THONGS
show more skin and create a longer line.

SLINGBACKS
can accentuate thick ankles by simply leaving too much exposed.

ANKLE STRAPS
can make ankles look thinner by giving them some definition. The added coverage on the heel helps, too.

ALWAYS
FLATTERING

HARD
TO
WEAR

pumps don't minimize the size of the foot

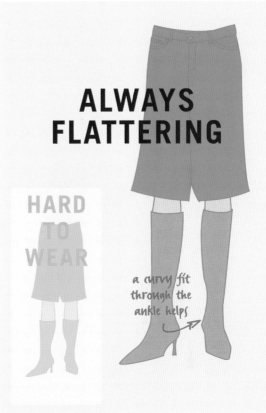

ALWAYS
FLATTERING

HARD
TO
WEAR

a curvy fit through the ankle helps

STRAPS
shorten the foot and make the leg look shorter, too.

CLASSIC PUMPS
strategically cover and reveal to improve the shape of the foot.

MID-CALF BOOTS
cut the lower leg at its widest spot, making it look shorter.

FITTED KNEE BOOTS
work to elongate your calves.

building a shoe closet

(2) PAIRS OF KNEE BOOTS

high-heel or kitten-heel or flat

(1) PAIR OF GOOD OFFICE SHOES

(1) PAIR OF EVENING SHOES

satin is nice

(1) PAIR OF CASUAL SHOES

IF THE SKY IS RAINING SHOES, ADD...

*whichever heel height you
don't already have*

ANOTHER PAIR OF KNEE BOOTS

*more comfortable
with pants*

ANKLE BOOTS

A FLAT OFFICE SHOE

building a shoe closet

(1) **PAIR OF GOOD FLAT SANDALS**

(2) **PAIRS OF GOOD OFFICE SHOES**

serious shoes that go with everything

high heel or mid-heel

(1) **PAIR OF FLIP-FLOPS**

(1) **PAIR OF STRAPPY, SEXY SANDAL**

IF THE SKY IS RAINING SHOES, ADD...

*fresh and trendy—
fabric or leather*

MORE FUN STRAPPY SANDALS

SOME LIGHT-COLORED OFFICE SHOES

wear it now, wear it later

Vivid peep-toes add an unexpected shot of color to a monochromatic tank-and-pencil-skirt ensemble.

PEEP-TOES

+

WINTER

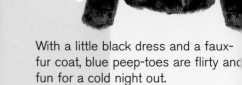

With a little black dress and a faux-fur coat, blue peep-toes are flirty and fun for a cold night out.

Versatile flats with a rich double-breasted coat and white jeans make for a clean-lined Parisian look.

SUMMER

In warm weather, wear flats with a casual dress, a summer bag, and pearl studs for a sweet-yet-sophisticated elegance.

BLACK FLATS

pick your favorites

OFFICE SHOES

| ANKLE-STRAP STILETTO | CANVAS+LEATHER SLINGBACK | PATENT PUMP | SPECTATOR D'ORSAY | STACK-HEEL PU |

FLAT SANDALS

| TRIMMED | BRAIDED T-STRAP | TOP-STITCHED | ANKLE STRAP | GROMMETED |

HIGH-HEEL SANDALS

| ANKLE-TIE | ANIMAL PRINT | STRAPPY | EMBELLISHED | MULE |

OFFICE SHOES

PUMP

FRINGE T-STRAP

MARY JANE

HIGH-HEEL LOAFER

ROUND TOE

EVENING SHOES

VELVET PUMP

TRIMMED
LEATHER

CRYSTAL
STUDDED

METALLIC

SATIN

BOOTS

WESTERN

ANKLE

EQUESTRIAN

FLAT

HIGH

3 pairs of shoes, 2 ways

STRAPPY SANDALS

CLASS

SURE...	BUT ALSO...	SURE...
SUNDRESS	**SILKY TOP + JEANS**	**VINTAGE JACKET + WOOL SKIRT**

the sandals dress up the jeans

BUT ALSO...

**TURTLENECK SWEATER
+
JEANS**

SURE...

**SWEATER
+
JEANS**

BUT ALSO...

**KHAKI JACKET
+
SUNDRESS**

*American
as apple pie*

*a funkier
look*

and you're Calamity Jane

Western boots are a classic, but with a full skirt, they're too costume-y. Think more cow*boy* than cow*girl*: you can't go wrong with a pair of great-fitting jeans.

OTHER OPTIONS

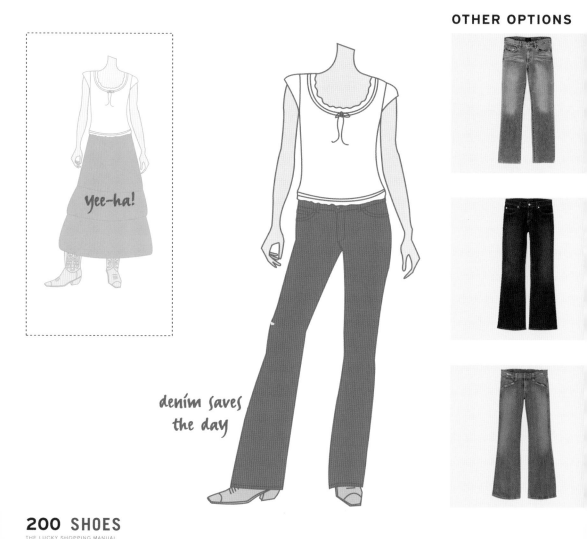

yee-ha!

denim saves
the day

WEAR THE RIGHT CLOTHES

If you know exactly what type of shoe you're looking for, dress appropriately when shopping: It's really hard to try on knee boots in jeans, or to get a good sense of how ankle boots will work if you're in a skirt. And try to get a look at yourself in a full-length mirror—shoe mirrors tell only half the story.

TAKE A WALK

Stroll around the store for a while, away from mirrors, so you can feel the shoes without seeing them. There are shoes other than high heels that are hard to walk in (and some heels can be surprisingly comfortable). Wood-bottom styles can feel harsh; in kitten heels, your weight is sometimes distributed in an awkward way; strappy sandals can be too light on straps, so pay attention.

HEED THE TINGLE

If you're experiencing a weird sensation that's not quite pain but is a far cry from comfort, skip the shoes. Shoes that induce strange feelings immediately are guaranteed to kill you after an eight-hour workday.

BE REALISTIC ABOUT SIZES

Go ahead and try a shoe a half size smaller or larger if your size is out of stock, but don't buy a pair unless you really think the fit is right; you'll end up never wearing them. Along the same lines, if you have wide feet, don't squeeze yourself into normal-width sandals. The edge of your foot will spill off the side, which looks awful, and you'll find yourself walking with part of your foot on the ground.

spend or save ?

Dressy designer shoes have a certain look to them, there's no doubt about it. But a lot of cheaper lines use the same factories, so you can get pretty good quality knock-offs for eveningwear. For quality, spend on boots; those that are made well really do look and fit better. Save on casual summer shoes, which tend to get trashed by the end of a season anyway.

CHAPTER 11

JACKETS

LADY JACKET

SHIRT JACKET

SUEDE

LEATHER

BLAZER

BOMBER

SAFARI

DENIM

MILITARY

fit and styling tips

1️⃣ PERFECT FIT

A fitted, three-button blazer with a mid-size lapel and a tapered waist is always flattering. Light-weight wool (or a comparable blend) with a little bit of stretch holds its shape best. Be sure the shoulder pads (they should be small) end right where your own shoulder ends. Wear the bottom or bottom two buttons open. Once you have the details down, it's all about fit.

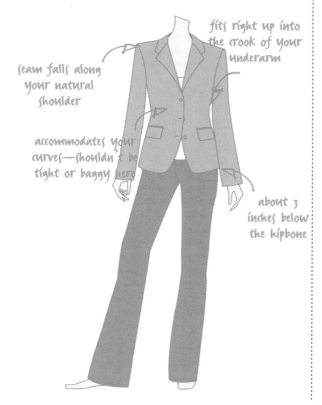

fits right up into the crook of your underarm

seam falls along your natural shoulder

accommodates your curves—shouldn't be tight or baggy here

about 3 inches below the hipbone

2️⃣ JACKETS WITH SKIRTS

Pairing jackets and skirts can be a bit tricky. The key is to look at the whole outfit and be sure that it shows enough of your own shape to flatter. Don't wear a classic fitted blazer with a loose, drapey skirt—or even an A-line skirt, because the overall shape is widening. A blazer needs the balance of a curve-hugging pencil skirt instead. Fuller skirts work with jackets that emphasize—and end at—your waist, like a bomber.

shape of the body is lost

curvy and flattering

THE CASE FOR BLAZERS

A blazer gives a certain polish to any look, casual or professional. If you have a job where you're frequently in suits, blazers offer a softer option, but still keep you covered in a meeting or when going to lunch.

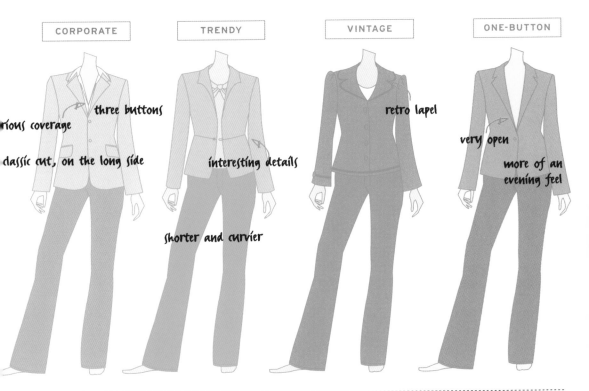

CORPORATE

three buttons

rious coverage

classic cut, on the long side

TRENDY

interesting details

shorter and curvier

VINTAGE

retro lapel

ONE-BUTTON

very open

more of an evening feel

HOW NOT TO LOOK BOYISH IN A BLAZER

If a blazer fits in a girly way—close to the body—you're halfway there. The next step is to dress it right. Don't combine a blazer with man-tailored styles like button-down shirts and trousers. Instead, add casual pieces like jeans, nice boots, a turtleneck, and feminine dangly earrings—or, for a work look, a pencil skirt and heels.

CHOOSING ALTERNATIVE TOPS

Mix things up a little when picking tops to wear under jackets, but use your head: don't wear a bat-wing top, because it will get all crumpled up. A very fitted jacket calls for a sleeveless top. Liven up a blazer with an interesting neckline, like an asymmetric shape or a boatneck. Neat, band-collar jackets look best with scoopnecks or turtlenecks.

the best jackets for you

BALANCE A PEAR-SHAPED BODY

ENHANCE SMALL BREASTS

strategically placed pockets help

FILL OUT SLOPED SHOULDERS

MAKE SHOULDERS SEEM SMALLER

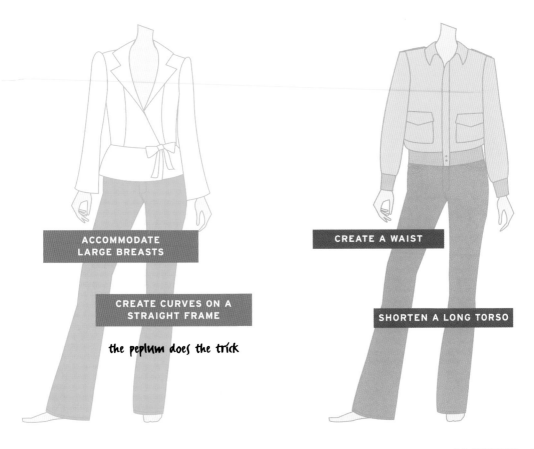

WEAR A '40S-STYLE FITTED BLAZER TO...

ACCOMMODATE LARGE BREASTS

CREATE CURVES ON A STRAIGHT FRAME

the peplum does the trick

WEAR A BOMBER JACKET TO...

CREATE A WAIST

SHORTEN A LONG TORSO

building a jacket closet

YOU'RE TOTALLY COVERED IF YOU HAVE...

(1) GOOD WOOL BLAZER

(1) SHORT JACKET

lightweight wool or a blend

(1) DENIM JACKET

YOU ALWAYS WEAR JACKETS TO WORK, ADD...

great on the street over skimpy clothes

A COUPLE MORE ALL-SEASON WOOL BLAZERS

A SUMMER BLAZER

for fall and winter

A VELVET BLAZER

any shape that works

A LIGHTWEIGHT SHORT JACKET

wear it now, wear it later

Pair a short jacket with tuxedo pants, sexy ankle boots, and a sleek bag for evening.

SHORT JACKET

For summer, it lightens up, topping off a ful pleated skirt and girly heels.

SUMMER

A fitted blazer instantly pulls together a summer work outfit.

WINTER

Throw it on over a turtleneck, jeans, and sleek shoe boots for a cozy, casual winter look.

BLAZER

3 jackets, 2 ways

CROPPED JACKET

MOTORCYC

WITH PANTS

MENSWEAR TROUSERS
+
POINTY-TOE PUMPS
+
CHUNKY RING

WITH A SKIRT

SUEDE A-LINE SKIRT
+
TWO-TONE T-STRAPS
+
DROP EARRINGS

WITH PANTS

STRETCH-CANVAS PANTS
+
LACE-UP ANKLE BOOTS

CKET

WITH A SKIRT

PRINT SKIRT
+
PEARLS
+
SATIN PUMPS

a

WITH PANTS

WIDE-WAISTBAND JEANS
+
POINTY BOOTS

WITH A SKIRT

PENCIL SKIRT
+
SUEDE CUT-OUT HEELS
+
LEATHER BAG

sexy detailing keeps things feminine

FASHION CHALLENGE:
jackets with dresses

The classic charm of leather and lace—like throwing on your boyfriend's jacket at the school dance.

A denim jacket dresses down chiffon and adds a waist to an unstructured, ethereal shape.

A jacket can change the personality of a dress, but the shapes have to be just right. Dresses with a defined waist need jackets with the same, or shorter jackets that don't interfere with the overall line.

A nightgown-drapey dress becomes a pretty skirt with a smart waist-defining belted jacket.

A belted, vintage-inspired jacket is a natural fit with a cinched sundress. Combined, they feel almost like a retro suit.

and you're Ally McBeal

The miniskirt-and-blazer look is only appropriate on TV. Much more sophisticated with a blazer is a sleek, mid-knee length pencil skirt; it strikes the perfect balance between sexy and professional.

OTHER OPTIONS

too much leg

a sleek work look

PENCIL SKIRT

JEANS

CIGARETTE PANTS

IN THE FITTING ROOM

WEAR THE
RIGHT TOP

Hit the racks for a couple of contrasting tops to try on with fashion-y blazers. Choose a conservative one—say, a simple thin sweater—and a fun one, with a drapey or asymmetric neckline. You never know where you might need your blazer to go.

KEEP YOUR
MIND OPEN

Minor alterations can be part of buying a blazer, but make sure you're happy with the basic styling. If you hate the lapel or if the front covers more of you than you'd like, look for another option. A blazer should look cool and sexy even before a tailor touches it.

BUTTON UP

Even though you'll wear your blazer open or with only the top button closed, you should fasten all buttons to check the fit. Focus on the things that are hard to change: shoulders and shoulder pads, underarm, and chest.

spend or save ?

Invest your money where fit is most critical—in a good wool blazer for work; it's very tough to find inexpensive blazers that fit well. A nice blazer will last for years, so you'll definitely get your money's worth. Save on a denim jacket; some of the less-expensive chains offer great choices in styling and detail, copied right from designer versions. You can also save on light cotton jackets—the less fitted they are, the easier it is to skimp.

eleanor lembo

JOB:
FASHION PR REP

STYLE:
EDGY EVENINGWEAR

HER RULES...

1 "Stick to classic evening dresses, and make them cool with funky accessories."

2 "Do a trend with integrity— by seeking out a vintage version of it."

3 "Don't underestimate the power of pulled-back hair and incredible earrings."

"THE MISTAKE PEOPLE make with black tie is thinking it's restrictive," says Eleanor Lembo, a native New Yorker and fixture on Manhattan's charity-benefit circuit. Lembo, who works in public relations for the jeans label Paper Denim and Cloth, adds a healthy dose of funkiness to eveningwear; instead of going designer head-to-toe, she'll throw distinct, fun, downtown pieces into the mix. "I might wear a Chanel dress," she says, "but I'll pair it with tall, tight suede boots, or legwarmers—something unexpected."

Lembo's anti-stuffy details make for outfits that are dressy enough to pass muster, yet entirely original. "The easiest way to individualize is through accessories—contemporary shoes, jewelry, a shawl," Lembo advises. "I once wore a black tassel tie—the kind you'd use to hold back a curtain—as a necklace with a formal dress." Because the dress was simple, she adds, "it worked."

That's part of Lembo's credo: Be creative with extras, but keep the backdrop classic. "A too-funky dress can make you feel uncomfortable," she says. "It's great to take chances, but do it in a subtler way—with a feather in your hair or a rocker-chick necklace."

One part Park Avenue, one part East Village, Lembo's evening look represents a range of influences: "I look to my mother for the traditional aspect and to the hipsters in my neighborhood for the edge," she says. The final product, though, is decidedly her own.

from eleanor's closet

VERSACE ENVELOPE BAG

"Even with the logo, it's cool because of the design. Reminds me of a '70s dress."

JIMMY CHOO WEDGES

"These go with anything— from an all-black dressy outfit to jeans."

"A birthday gift from my best friend."

CHANEL DRESS

DANGLY EARRINGS

"Supercheap rocker-style earrings I bought on the street."

MY FAVORITES:

DESIGNER (for eveningwear): Chanel, Balenciaga, Chloé, Dior

SHOES "Marc Jacobs black leather boots that are a few years old and falling apart."

JEANS Paper Denim and Cloth

HIGH-END STORES Barneys New York and Eva (on Mulberry Street in Manhattan). "I always go there first when I'm looking for a dress."

MAINSTREAM STORE H&M

FASHION ERA '70s

FASHION ICON Audrey Hepburn

COLOR TO WEAR Muted tones, "like gray-blue and dirty pink"

TALL SUEDE BO

"I might wear these with a Chanel or Ralph Lauren dress for a black-tie event."

BEADED RALPH LAUREN SKIRT

"Nice for a dressy party, with a white or light-blue polo top."

ANTIQUE DIAMOND EARRINGS

"The kind of earrings that can make the look— just pull back your hair, and you're done."

J. MENDEL DRESS

"There are times when everyone is wearing black, so his almost feels wild—I love how colorful and festive it is."

TIERED DRESS

"Just my kind of thing— edgy but not too look-at-me outrageous."

SPIDER HEELS

"I like things with an extra detail, like the jeweled stone here."

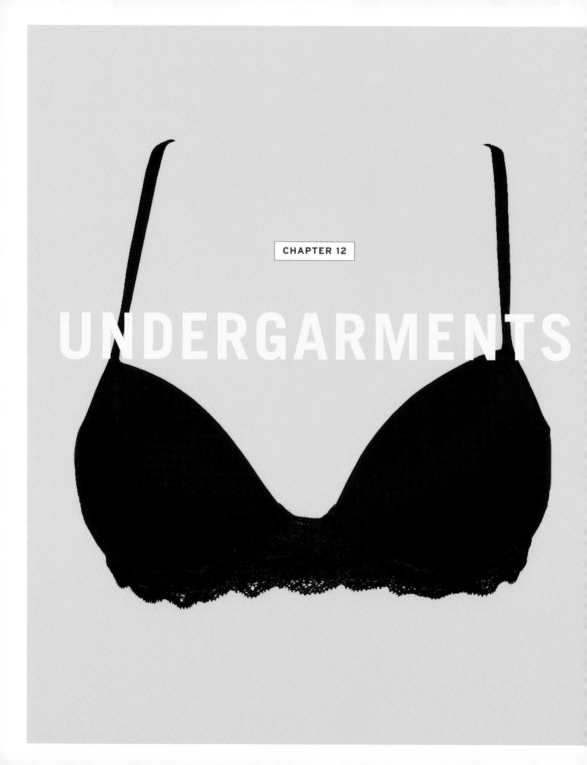

CHAPTER 12

UNDERGARMENTS

ENHANCING BRA

HIP BRIEFS

SOFT-CUP BRA

STRETCHY CAMISOLE

DEMI-CUP BRA

CONVERTIBLE BRA

BIKINI

BOY BRIEFS

TAP PANTS

THONG

MOLDED-CUP BRA

SILK CAMISOLE

FULL SLIP

HALF SLIP

FRONT-CLOSE BRA

FISHNETS

fit and styling tips: undergarments

1 PAY ATTENTION TO YOUR UNDERWEAR

Sure, sexy lingerie is fun, but practical undergarments are worth a little investment. Perfectly smooth underpants will make all your clothes look better, and a great-fitting bra will do more for your figure than anything you might wear over it. When shopping for both bras and panties, be conservative: if you find an item you think is right, buy only one (not several). After some wear and washings, if you're still happy with the fit—and if the elastic has held up well—go back and stock up.

not the look you're after

2 BUY SILKY BRAS

For everyday use, limit yourself to smooth, slippery bras, because they work best under all tops. Some tops don't fall well over cotton bras— there's just too much friction. Save pretty, impractical bras, like lace (the texture can show through) and velvet (a static nightmare) for after-hours.

3 ELIMINATE PANTY LINES

Good-quality, seamless, low-cut briefs that fit right under your butt will give you a smooth line under any clothes. Thongs have problems: They often peek out of your pants; and actually give you panty lines in some clothes like thin, silky dresses. Whatever style you choose, be sure that your underpants stay under your waistline and always have a cotton crotch.

4 YOU DON'T NEED A WHITE BRA

To keep your bra invisible, don't match the color of the shirt; match the color of your sk Almost all your bras should be nude. Get or black bra with skinny straps to wear with skimpy black tops; nude straps showing fro under a black top can look kind of matronly

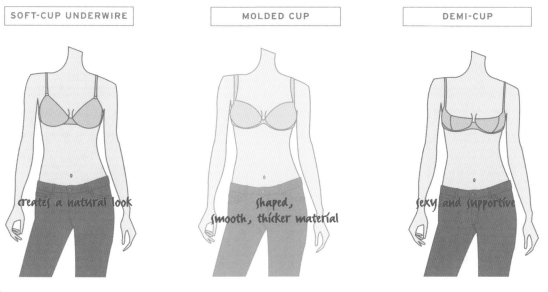

| SOFT-CUP UNDERWIRE | MOLDED CUP | DEMI-CUP |

creates a natural look

shaped, smooth, thicker material

sexy and supportive

KNOW YOUR BRA OPTIONS

If you're a B-cup or bigger, you should wear an underwire bra: soft-cup under-wires provide some support and give a natural, unsculpted line. Full-coverage, molded-cup underwires are smooth and provide a professional look, but they can be stiff. Demi-cups, which leave the top of the breast revealed, are available in soft- or molded-cup versions and almost always include underwires.

ENHANCING BRAS CAN BE TOO MUCH

For all but those with the smallest busts, enhancing bras can easily go overboard and create an unnatural look. Be sure that you're getting the effect you want and not more than you bargained for. To keep your silhouette within the realm of reality, choose push-up action or padding—but not both.

7 AVOIDING BRA TROUBLE

T-shirts show every little thing that's underneath them. Don't wear a demi-cup bra with a tee because it can cut you horizontally and make you look like you have four breasts. Stay away from padded bras with T-shirts if you're small-breasted, because they look fake. And be sure to wear a bra that's low enough in the armpit not to show under tanks.

fit and styling tips: hosiery

1 HOSE AND STOCKINGS

The ideal hose give legs a finished look without adding color. Go with the sheerest kind you can find—almost clear; avoid hose that give you a "tan" or make legs shine (though if you like sheer black hose for evening, a little shimmer is nice). For a really special night, you might want to opt for old-fashioned stockings and a garter belt; stockings are less confining and way sexier. Check lingerie shops for garter belt hose, a modern one-piece version with no hardware. Don't forget that bare legs are also very chic, if you can get away with them (carefully applied self-tanner can be as good as hose), and they afford you the option of open-toe shoes.

thickening   flattering

2 PATTERNED TIGHTS

Stick with subtly patterned tights, like her-ringbone, for a sophisticated look. Wide stripes or polka dots can be juvenile, unless they're part of a bigger statement. Cable-knit tights, with a high added-bulk factor, also belong on people with single-digit ages. Stick with understated vertical pat-terns that peek out between skirt hem and boot top. Steer clear of horizontal designs, which make legs look thicker.

3 SOLID TIGHTS

Look for matte tights (cotton or a blend) with a small percentage of Lycra; too much stretch makes you reflect light like an ice skater. Wearing tights with a mini and boots can help lengthen the line of your legs—especially when you stick with black boots and black tights. Avoid major color contrasts, which can have the opposite effect.

FISHNETS

Risky as they might seem, fishnets are flattering on most people. Get a good-quality pair with a smooth, solid reinforced seat—because under clingy clothes, the outline of fishnet on your hips can show through. Skip the kind with the seam up the back; it's too much work to keep them straight. Wear fishnets at night with a '40s-style dress, a denim skirt, or as part of a ladylike look, with a knee-length skirt and vintage-y shoes. Fishnets are also great against a conservative outfit, but keep them away from busy patterned pieces. If you feel shy about wearing the real thing, try a pair of fishnet-print hose, which give the illusion of holes without showing any actual skin.

 ## WOOL TIGHTS

Because they can look a bit school-girlish, wool tights are tricky. Pair them with something feminine but grown up, like a fitted wool dress. Buy the thinnest wool tights you can find because, like anything that's textured, they can add weight to your legs; combat this further with not-too-dressy heels, like loafer-style pumps. Skip wool tights altogether if you have chunky legs; they'll make them look chunkier.

how to fit a bra

Start from scratch to make sure you're wearing the right size. Then check each detail so you know you're getting the best fit possible.

STEP 1:
LEARN YOUR SIZE

Measure around the top of your ribs, right where your breasts meet your ribcage. Pull the tape tight around your back. Add five inches to this measurement, and you have the number part of your bra size. (So if your ribcage measures 29 inches, you're a size 34.) Now run the tape measure from the inside of your sternum (right between the breasts) to just outside the edge of one breast. Four inches roughly equals an A cup; five inches, a B cup; six inches, a C; and so on.

STEP 2:
TRY ON EVERYTHING

Even when you know your correct size, don't just pull a bra off the rack and buy it. Bra cuts vary wildly, and their tags don't include subtle info like "full side cup" or "broader through the back." These are the little differences that make one bra fit perfectly and another not.

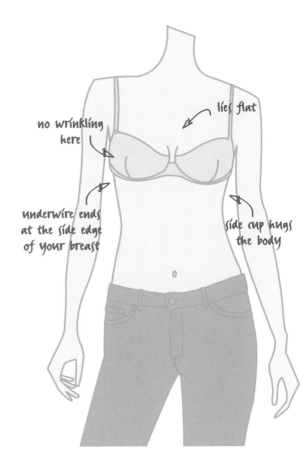

no wrinkling here

lies flat

underwire ends at the side edge of your breast

side cup hugs the body

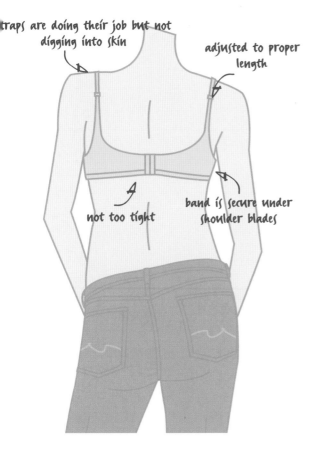

traps are doing their job but not digging into skin

adjusted to proper length

not too tight

band is secure under shoulder blades

STEP 3:
CHECK THE FIT

In a well-fitting bra, your breasts will completely fill the cups (in soft cups, check the tip, especially; in molded bras, be sure that the top of the cups are filled out). Cups should hug the outer edges of your breasts, and the back band should be anchored under the lowest part of your shoulder blades. Last of all, the short piece of fabric between the breasts should lie flat against your body.

the best bra for the job

DEFINE BREASTS WITH...

GIVE BREASTS A BOOST WITH...

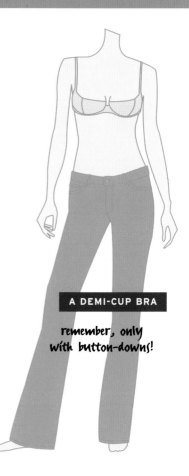

A MOLDED-CUP BRA

lots of support and no nipple show-through

A DEMI-CUP BRA

remember, only with button-downs!

AN ENHANCING BRA

...lls up and in, and pads
you from below

A MINIMIZER

sturdy fabric, plus wide back and
shoulder straps, do the trick

building an undergarment drawer

YOU'RE TOTALLY COVERED IF YOU HAVE...

⑦ PAIRS OF EVERYDAY UNDERPANTS

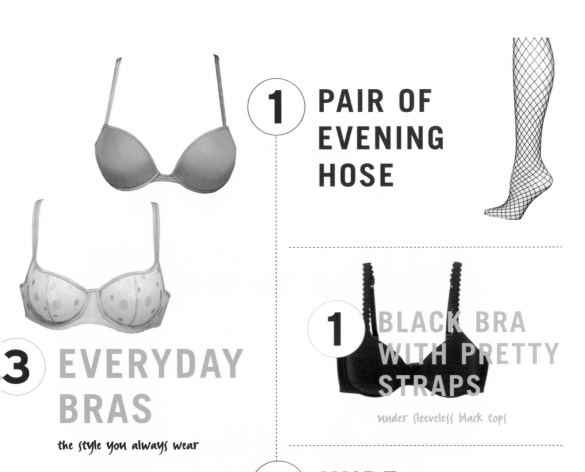

1 PAIR OF EVENING HOSE

3 EVERYDAY BRAS

the style you always wear

1 BLACK BRA WITH PRETTY STRAPS

under sleeveless black tops

1 NUDE STRETCHY CAMISOLE

for sheer tops

building an undergarment drawer

(1) **SILKY CAMISOLE**
with lace trim you can show off
under V-necks

(1) PAIR OF THIN
WOOL TIGHTS
FOR WINTER
solid or tweedy

(1) CONVERTIBLE
BRA
switches to a halter or
strapless, as needed

AS MANY
PAIRS OF
WORK HOSE
AS YOU NEED

(1) CUTE SET TO
SLEEP IN

IF YOU WANT TO BE READY FOR ANYTHING, ADD...

ANOTHER EVERYDAY BRA

SOME FUN BRAS

ANOTHER SILKY CAMISOLE

cotton or silk

SOME THIN, FITTED TANKS FOR LAYERING

if nothing else, sleep in it

A FULL SLIP

for the skirt that always sticks to your legs

A HALF SLIP

STOCKINGS AND A GARTER BELT

what to wear under what

**DEMI-CUP BRA
+
OPEN BLOUSE**

*lets you unbutton
low*

**MOLDED-CUP BRA
OR SOFT-CUP UNDERWIRE
+
T-SHIRT**

*depends which look
you like*

**NUDE BRA
+
WHITE TOP**

*white under white shows
through; nude doesn't*

SKINNY-STRAP
FULL-COVERAGE BRA
+
CLINGY TANK

so you don't feel naked

ATHLETIC BRA
+
RACERBACK TANK

no straps peeking out

PRETTY-STRAP BRA
+
SLIP-OFF-THE-SHOULDER
SWEATER

it's okay if it shows

what to wear under what

STRAPLESS BRA
+
SPAGHETTI-STRAP PARTY
DRESS

the fitted bodice
helps keep the bra up

LACE-TRIMMED BOY
SHORTS
+
LIGHT SUMMER DRESS

in case it's
windy

FRONT-CLOSURE BRA
+
PLUNGING NECKLINE

the lowest option

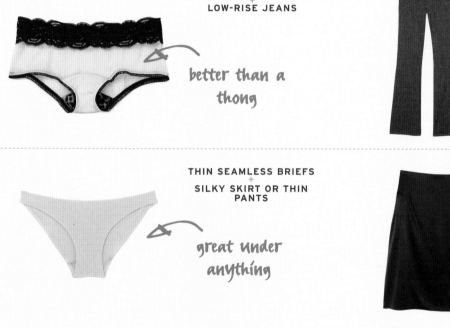

**LOW-RISE BRIEFS
+
LOW-RISE JEANS**

*better than a
thong*

**THIN SEAMLESS BRIEFS
+
SILKY SKIRT OR THIN
PANTS**

*great under
anything*

**FISHNETS
+
OPEN-TOE SHOES**

*bare legs look
great, too*

and you're in a "Girls Gone Wild" video

Sheer, chiffony tops beg the world to look at your underwear. A stretchy camisole close to your skin tone, decent enough to be worn on its own, always has you covered.

OTHER OPTIONS

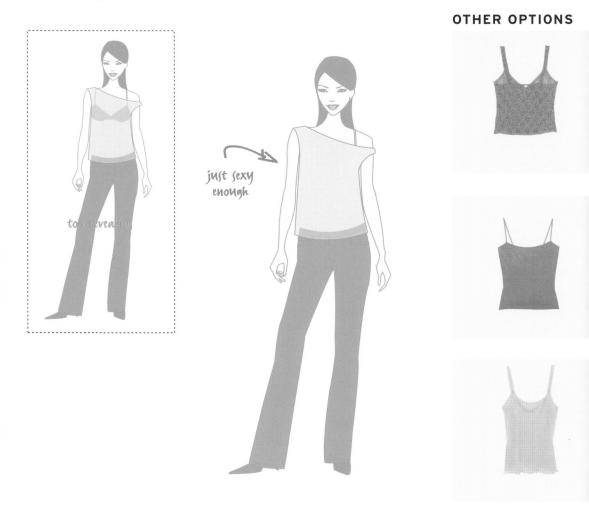

just sexy enough

top revealing

IN THE FITTING ROOM

POUR AND SHAKE

Putting on a bra is not as simple as, well, putting on a bra. To get yourself situated properly, you have to pour yourself into the cups: Once the straps are on, lean forward and slip breasts into the cups, then shake a little to settle yourself in before you fasten.

PUT YOUR TOP ON

Once you've found a bra with a good fit, slip on a top (be sure to wear the right one to the store). It's easy to get caught up in fit details and lose sight of overall shape. Sometimes what looks like bra perfection when you're shirtless can be kind of '50s bullet-breast when you're dressed.

SIT DOWN

When you sit or slouch in a molded-cup bra, the top of the cups can stand away from the breasts, and suddenly you're not filling out the cups anymore. Try a molded cup with less coverage, instead.

GET THE BACK RIGHT

If a standard-closure bra bows up in back, try lengthening the straps or going up a size (in number, not letter). If that doesn't help, a front-closure style might work better on your body and solve the problem.

spend or save ?

A silk camisole is worth the money, because synthetic versions just don't compare to the feel of the real thing. You don't have to spend a fortune on one (what you'd get if you did is finer-quality lace); just hit the department stores. Save your money on panty hose, because even the really pricey ones can rip the first time you wear them. Hose are best thought of as disposable.

THE LUCKY SHOPPING MANUAL

LUCKY GIRL

brooke williams

JOB:
PHOTOGRAPHER &
MUSICIAN

STYLE:
ECLECTIC CLASSIC

HER RULES...

1 "Dress around your day and be comfortable."

2 "Wear happy clothes to brighten the world."

3 "Don't leave the house without your signature jewelry."

4 "Stop by the Salvation Army in every town you visit."

PHOTOGRAPHER AND MUSICIAN

Brooke Williams leads an enviably colorful life. Shooting portraits, composing melancholic tunes, performing at downtown Manhattan clubs—this is the stuff of her day. And her eclectic wardrobe reflects the richness and variety of her artsy existence.

Williams combines pieces that might otherwise never meet (say, a rock T-shirt and a golf skirt), and she delivers a whole new take on outfits meant to match: "I'm a big men's suit fan, especially the kind from the '60s, with straight legs," she says.

Vintage finds and her "huge, sentimental T-shirt collection" are augmented with new pieces—everything from Vivienne Westwood to L.L. Bean. "I tend to stick to classics when I buy new," she says. "I choose pieces that will last."

A touch of glamour comes in the form of high-end shoes, like Gucci and Prada, "from the sample sales," she adds. "My whole shopping situation is thrift stores and sample sales."

One of the things that makes Williams stand out is her refreshing take on color. She embraces bright shades and playful prints, and says some choices can have a tangible effect on her mood. "I think of it as dressing happy," she explains. "Sometimes I'll just say to myself, I'm going to wear my watermelon-print dress, and maybe that will make it a better day."

from brooke's closet

LACOSTE SWEATER

"I was super-preppie growing up, so I have a nostalgic attachment to all things Lacoste."

JILL PLATNER JEWELRY

"Most of the jewelry I wear is by Jill Platner; it's handmade and organic-looking."

"I like '60s straight-leg men's suits. I'll find one at a vintage store that sort of fits, then take it to a tailor."

MEN'S SUIT

MEN'S PLAID CUT-OFFS

"In summer, I live in these. I'm in search of a seamstress to have them copied before they fall apart."

MY FAVORITES:

DESIGNER Benjamin Cho.
"I was waiting to have a reason to order something from him. Then I got engaged and ordered my wedding dress. It's the only piece of his I own."

SHOES "My purple Adidas."

JEANS "I only wear Levi's. They fit really well, and they're the jeans I've always worn."

HIGH-END STORES
"I don't really shop at high-end stores."

MAINSTREAM STORE Salvation Army

FASHION ERA Mid-'60s

FASHION ICON Emma Peel, of the *Avengers*

COLORS TO WEAR
White, green, and orange

GOLF SKIRT

"The print is slightly abstract and graphic, s• it's not like you're walki•• around with a cheesy, goofy pattern."

CHECKED COAT

"The lining is an incredible ZigZag, so it's a cacaphony of patterns."

FAUX FUR HAT

"The greatest, warmest, most excellent hat— and it makes people on the street smile. I don't know how people survive in normal little hats. This one is 16 inches across."

KURTIS BLOW T-SHIRT

"One of my favorite rappers when I was a kid. I've had this since I was about 13."

KURTIS BLOW

YVES SAINT LAURENT SKIRT

"An early '80s skirt from my friend's sidewalk sale. It looks potentially matronly but fits really well, so it's shapely without being slutty."

CHAPTER 13

SWIMWEAR

BOY SHORTS

TANK

HALTER

ATHLETIC

STRING BIKINI

ONE-SHOULDER

BANDEAU

KEYHOLE

SHIRRED

TANKINI

METALLIC

CUTOUT

fit and styling tips

built for speed

fun and still swimmable

crochet is hot, but about as practical as stilettos at a picnic

① PERFECT FIT

Here's a situation where it's really important not to stress out about the number on the tag. Focus only on how the suit looks and feels on your body. Half of looking great in a swimsuit is getting the fit right, so if you're shopping for a two-piece, make it easy on yourself and buy separates, which let you get exactly what you need—in terms of both fit and cut—for each half.

② LET THE ACTIVITY DICTATE THE SUIT

There are some swimsuits meant just for posing by the pool, others intended for serious athletics, and many, many in between. You don't want to swim laps in a string bikini, but a two-piece with a dependable stay-put top will serve you well on the sand and among the waves. Be practical about fabrics, too; for example, a crochet bikini might be cool, but it will take hours to dry after you've been swimming.

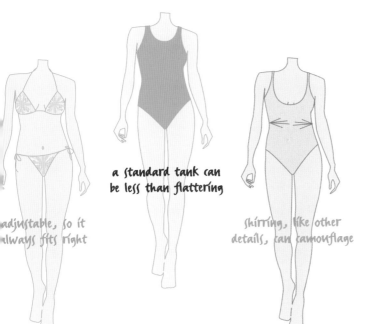

a standard tank can
be less than flattering

adjustable, so it
always fits right

shirring, like other
details, can camouflage

3. TRY ON STYLES YOU THINK YOU CAN'T WEAR

A string bikini may seem like the most unforgiving of swimsuits, but because it's adjustable it never cuts into your skin. Even if you're not superskinny (though you do need to be somewhat firm), this style can be flattering. Less revealing two-pieces, like athletic suits and tankinis, can often look better than a plain one-piece tank, because a two-piece breaks up that solid mass of color. For the same reason, one-piece suits with a little something going on—shirring, a pretty pattern, or a belt—can be a better option than an unadorned tank. The point is, you never know what might work until you see it on your body.

shades of Aunt Sadie

looks good

4. HOW TO MAKE YOUR BUTT LOOK ITS BEST

One advantage to buying swimwear separates is that you can customize butt coverage with a slightly larger size. But too much modesty can work against you. Full coverage can make your butt look bigger—even matronly. Revealing a bit of cheek is more flattering.

fit and styling tips

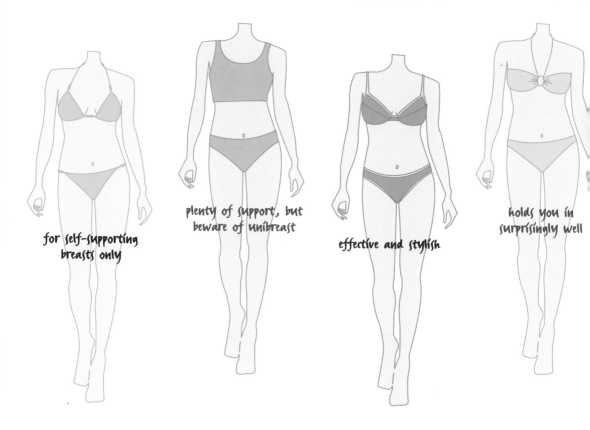

for self-supporting
breasts only

plenty of support, but
beware of unibreast

effective and stylish

holds you in
surprisingly well

⑤ THE STYLE/SUPPORT BALANCE POINT

Be realistic about how much support you need in a swimsuit top, and shop accordingly. Triangle tops are for very firm breasts only; otherwise they can have a flattening effect. The super-supportive athletic top has its own issues: if it's too small, it can give you unibreast. Like all swimsuit tops, it should contain without being confining. Underwire tops are great because they offer extra support without sacrificing style, but molded-cup versions can look a bit old-lady. The sexy keyhole top—as long as it has substantial straps and a metal ring at its center—offers support from many directions, and therefore can be a particularly smart choice.

6 THE BOY SHORT MYTH

In the abstract, boy shorts might seem easy to wear—less revealing should translate into more flattering, right? In this case, wrong. Because they cut your leg straight across rather than at an upward angle, boy shorts actually make your hips and butt look bigger. Cute as they are, they work best on the very narrowest figures.

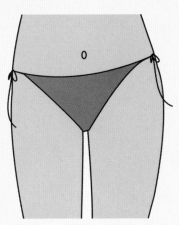

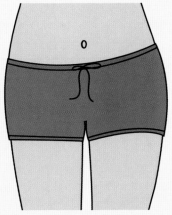

best if you have no hips

7 RETHINK COLORS

We all know that black clothes are slimming; it's natural to be drawn to black swimwear for the same reason. But if you're fair-skinned, the contrast doesn't do you any favors. Give some thought to alternate colors in swimwear, and choose those that flatter your skin tone. If you're really fair, a rich brown or muted blue will work better than black. You could also consider opening up your color options with carefully applied self-tanner, which offers the added bonus of camouflaging imperfections.

8 STICK WITH PROVEN LABELS

If you have a swimsuit that fits really well, it makes sense to return to the source when you need another; you'll have the best luck with labels that you know work for you. And if swimwear shopping makes you self-critical, skip the sale rack. Odds are that whatever's hanging there looked terrible on a lot of other women, so why put yourself through it?

the best swimsuits for you

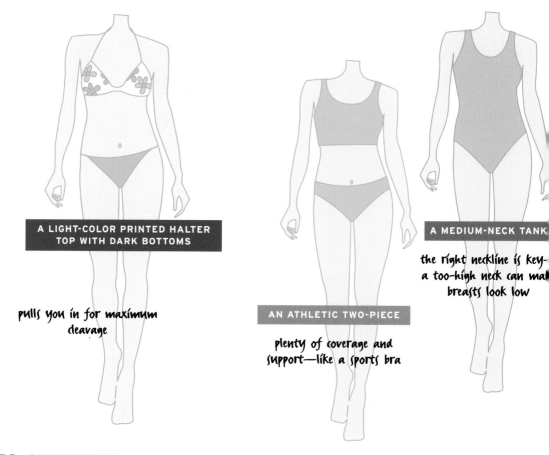

ENHANCE SMALL BREASTS WITH...

A LIGHT-COLOR PRINTED HALTER TOP WITH DARK BOTTOMS

pulls you in for maximum cleavage

MINIMIZE LARGE BREASTS WITH...

AN ATHLETIC TWO-PIECE

plenty of coverage and support—like a sports bra

A MEDIUM-NECK TANK

the right neckline is key—a too-high neck can make breasts look low

ACCOMMODATE LOVE HANDLES WITH...

A STRING BIKINI

tied to fit, it's surprisingly flattering

MINIMIZE HIPS WITH...

A V-BOTTOM

magically slimming

BREAK UP A LONG TORSO WITH...

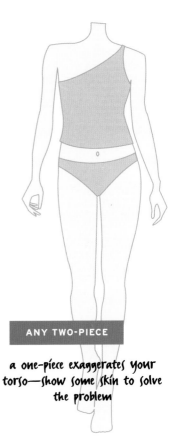

ANY TWO-PIECE

a one-piece exaggerates your torso—show some skin to solve the problem

the best swimsuits for you

HIDE A BELLY WITH...

A SHIRRED ONE-PIECE

LOOK SLIMMER ALL OVER WITH...

CHEVRON STRIPES

MAKE THIGHS LOOK LONGER WITH...

A HIGHCUT LEG

medium-high is actually more lengthening than super-high

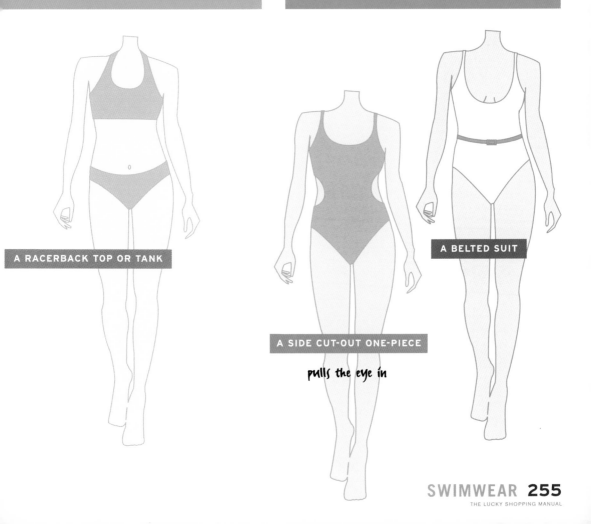

BROADEN SLOPED SHOULDERS WITH...

CREATE A WAIST WITH...

A RACERBACK TOP OR TANK

A SIDE CUT-OUT ONE-PIECE

pulls the eye in

A BELTED SUIT

building a swimsuit drawer

YOU'RE TOTALLY COVERED IF YOU HAVE...

2 ## SWIMMABLE SUITS

1 ## TOP COVER-UP
long-sleeve for sun protection

1 ## BOTTOM COVER-UP
for the walk to the snack bar

TO FILL OUT YOUR FANTASY-VACATION SUITCASE, ADD...

just for posing

ONE BATHING BEAUTY SUIT

MORE COVER-UPS

one for every day of the trip

MORE SWIMMABLE SUITS

pick your favorites

ONE-PIECE

TW

DIAGONAL-STRIPE HALTER

LACE-RUFFLE HALTER

BOY-LEG

'50S-PRINT BANDEA

FLORAL PEEPHOLE

BANDEAU

COLORBLOCK METALLIC

BASIC BIKINI

TEENY BIKINI

STRING TANKINI

BOLD-PRINT

BELTED SUEDE

JEWELED

BOY-SHORT BIKINI

BATIK

TEXTURED

ONE-TIE

four total beach looks

BOHEMIAN

BATIK BIKINI
+
COWBOY HAT
+
PRINTED SARONG

the cover-up doubles as a beach blanket

SPORTY

STRIPED TANKINI
+
TERRY CLOTH HOODIE

functional but fun

PREPPY

BOY-SHORT TWO-PIECE
+
MADRAS SHIRT
+
ETHNIC THONGS

a clean mix of brights and muted tones

GLAMOROUS

HALTER BIKINI
+
SILK SLIPDRESS
+
JEWELED THONGS

rich details add a movie star edge

mixing swimwear separates

This appliqué top and print bottom mix doubly well, because they share both a palette and a boho vibe.

Stripes—wide and narrow— plus a subtle sailor flair, bring a bright halter and belted bottom together.

These pieces couldn't be further apart in personality, but the pink and green in both make them a viable combo.

Tops and bottoms are sold separately so you can get the right fit, but the added benefit is you can create custom combinations. Choose bottoms that pick up a single color or the general personality of the top.

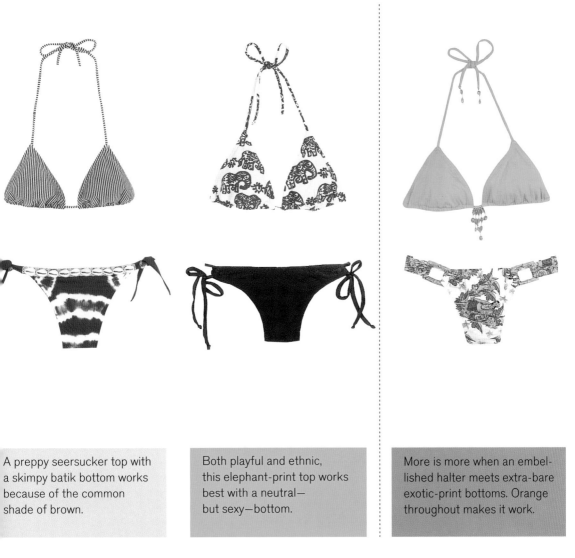

A preppy seersucker top with a skimpy batik bottom works because of the common shade of brown.

Both playful and ethnic, this elephant-print top works best with a neutral— but sexy—bottom.

More is more when an embellished halter meets extra-bare exotic-print bottoms. Orange throughout makes it work.

and you're Dynasty-era Joan Collins

The St. Tropez look can get out of hand when you top off a glam suit and glittery slides with a giant sunhat. Take it down a peg with a simple, understated bucket hat.

OTHER OPTIONS

MOD

CHIC

SPORTY

IN THE FITTING ROOM

BEND, STRETCH, AND SQUAT

Move as much as you can when trying on a swimsuit (just think how vigorously you use your body when you swim), to see if the seat rides up. Don't buy one that needs constant yanking down.

CHECK FOR CUTTING AND PULLING

If elastic is digging in anywhere—butt or back or shoulders—this is not the right suit for you. Also, look out if a one-piece suit doesn't conform to the curve of your spine but instead stands away from your lower back. It's probably too small.

IGNORE THE LIGHTING

Department-store fitting rooms are notorious for their bad lighting. If you see cellulite along the back of your thigh that you've never seen at home, it's probably not going to be visible at the pool, where flat, blinding sunlight works in your favor.

SHOP AT HOME

The most luxurious (and productive) way to shop for swimwear is to order a pile of options from a catalog or Website and try them on in the comfort—and natural light—of your own home. This will give you a realistic approximation of what you'll actually look like on the beach. Take your time deciding, then send back the suits you don't want.

---

spend or save ?

There's no need to spend a lot on a swimsuit. But an expensive suit that might be worth the splurge is one with special (and obviously costly) design elements, like a metal-ring keyhole or a cutout pattern. Skip pricey versions of simple styles; there are plenty of mid-range and even inexpensive options available that are close enough. And save money on trendy suits, which you can find cheap at some department stores or hip chain stores; the elastic may make it through only one or two seasons—but for a trendy style, that's just right.

THE LUCKY SHOPPING MANUAL

marlien rentmeester

JOB:
FASHION EDITOR

STYLE:
VINTAGE MODERN

HER RULES...

1 "Wear neutrals, and add one colorful accessory."

2 "Choose vintage pieces that don't scream a certain era."

3 "Save schlumpy clothes for the gym—dressing up is fun."

AS LUCKY'S WEST COAST editor, it's Marlien Rentmeester's job to spot L.A. fashion trends before anyone else. What makes her personal style sparkle is how she melds the edgy looks she uncovers with pretty vintage pieces for an elegance all her own.

"I love delicate, lacy clothes, but worn with a modern attitude," says Rentmeester. In her closet, filmy vintage blouses commingle with designer items (Marc by Marc Jacobs and Cynthia Rowley) and what Rentmeester calls her "stalwart staples": black turtlenecks, V-necks, and tailored trousers. "Assembling a great outfit is a game for me," she says. "I like experimenting—digging out old pieces and trying them with something new and fun."

Drawn to contrasting shapes, Rentmeester might pair a fitted black turtleneck with a pink lace A-line skirt and stilettos—or wear a blousy vintage top (her favorite is one purchased by her mother at a Jakarta flea market) with slim black trousers. "The effect," she says, "should not be too girly—definitely street smart."

A transplanted New Yorker, Rentmeester loves a chic, finished look—and she doesn't bend on that, even though she's switched to the more casual coast. "Everyone here wears T-shirts and flip flops," she says. "I like to dress up. I'm probably the only woman in L.A. who wears heels to the supermarket."

"Great with kitten heels or with flats, so I can go to work, switch my shoes, and wear them to dinner."

TRACY FEITH SHEER TOP

MANOLO BLAHNIKS

"Extremely wearable because of the low heel, but still elegant. I love the color combination."

MARC JACOBS CROPPED CARGO PANTS

"So unique and retro. I love it because it looks vintage, but it's not."

MY FAVORITES:

DESIGNER Marc Jacobs

SHOES "My green and purple Manolos . They're so different and decadent and colorful, but still wearable."

JEANS Moto

HIGH-END STORES Harvey Nichols and Barneys New York

MAINSTREAM STORE Gap

FASHION ERA Now

FASHION ICON "That's hard. Maybe Kate Moss meets Jackie O."

COLOR TO WEAR Black and pink, "not necessarily together"

"I'm the queen of lace—I wear this with a brooch at the base of the V-neck, so it looks like old lingerie."

TRACY REESE LACE TOP

FRENCH SOLE CANVAS FLATS

"Ballet flats are a wardrobe staple for me."

VINTAGE DRESS

"I stole this perfect nighttime dress from my twin sister—a great flea-market find."

DENIM JACKET

"Looks like a fancy blazer, but it's denim, so it works everywhere"

MOTO JEANS

"From Top Shop in London. These fit me better than any jeans ever. They seem to actually shrink my butt a size."

LACE BLOUSE

"My mother's beautiful blouse. It has no buttons, so I fasten it with a brooch."

CHAPTER 14

OUTERWEAR

PEACOAT

.TRENCH

BELTED OVERCOAT

WINDBREAKER

LEATHER JACKET

PUFFER

VINTAGE

TOGGLE

SHEARLING

fit and styling tips

① PERFECT OVERCOAT

Your overcoat is probably more important than any other single piece of clothing; you'll wear it on winter workdays for years. So choose a classic style, like a long, belted wool coat, in a flattering neutral shade. Look for shoulders that fit well (structured but not heavily padded); non-trendy mid-size lapels; and on-seam pockets. Use hats, scarves, and footwear for color and personality, but keep your coat subtle and sophisticated.

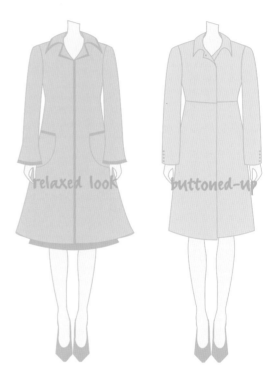

relaxed look   buttoned-up

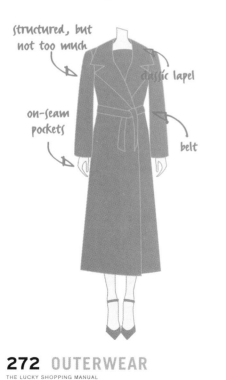

structured, but not too much

classic lapel

on-seam pockets

belt

② LET YOUR SKIRT SHOW

It's fine for a skirt or dress to peek out of the bottom of your coat, as long as the overall look is loose—say, a casual flowy skirt with flat boots. But a neat A-line or pencil skirt worn with a tailored coat should be fully covered, à la Jackie O.

4 DOUBLE- VS. SINGLE-BREASTED STYLING

A double-breasted coat has that impressive military crispness, but it can be hard to wear because it adds an extra layer. In coats, a layer is substantial, so if you're short, big-busted, or you just don't feel you can get away with additional bulk, stick with a single-breasted cut.

3 HOW TO WEAR A TRENCH

A trench can be a nice professional option for rain or transitional weather, but a traditional version runs the risk of looking severe and secret-agent-like. Instead of paying big bucks for an unflattering classic, shop trendier stores for a girly, tailored trench. Choose as shorter style that doesn't cover up your whole outfit so you don't get that flasher effect. And think about lightening up the look with a color rather than a neutral. Overall, you're going more for Audrey Hepburn than Inspector Gadget.

5 AN UNEXPECTED SOURCE

Vintage stores are a great source for unique dressy coats. Look for leopard-print, velvet, and fun fur in classic shapes that don't scream any specific era. Skip coats with moth holes, heavy smells, or seriously damaged linings.

the best coats for you

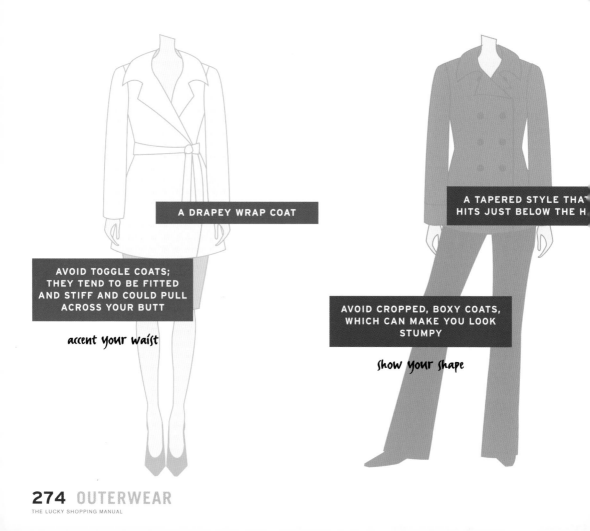

A DRAPEY WRAP COAT

AVOID TOGGLE COATS; THEY TEND TO BE FITTED AND STIFF AND COULD PULL ACROSS YOUR BUTT

accent your waist

A TAPERED STYLE THA" HITS JUST BELOW THE H

AVOID CROPPED, BOXY COATS, WHICH CAN MAKE YOU LOOK STUMPY

show your shape

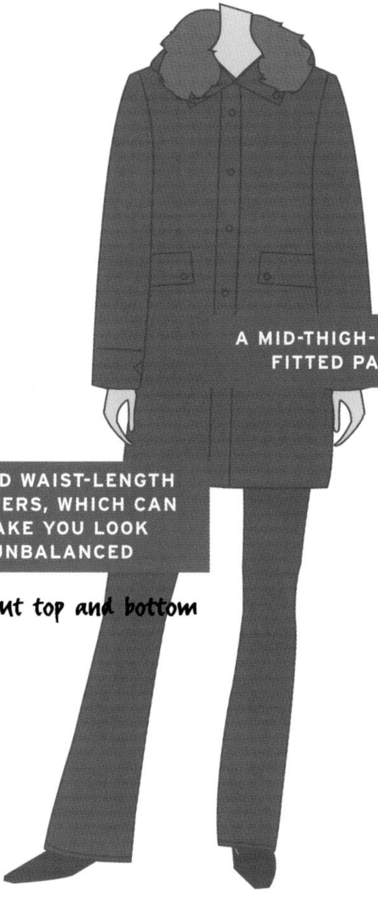

A MID-THIGH-LENGTH
FITTED PARKA

A CLASSIC BELTED
OVERCOAT WILL WORK
FOR YOU

VOID WAIST-LENGTH
UFFERS, WHICH CAN
MAKE YOU LOOK
UNBALANCED

long and lengthening

s out top and bottom

building an outerwear closet

YOU'RE TOTALLY COVERED IF YOU HAVE...

1 WARM PARKA
long enough to cover your hips

1 SPRING JACKET
any shape that flatters you

1 OVERCOAT
classic styling

1 RAINCOAT
functional but fun

1 FALL COAT

IF YOU LIVE IN MINNESOTA, ADD...

AN EVENING COAT

SOME FUN COATS

A LIGHTWEIGHT, CASUAL JACKET

pick your favorites

SLIGHTLY TAPERED

SHAGGY & COTTON

WOOL

PARKAS

FLANNEL-LINED

FULL COVERAGE

REAL-FUR HOOD

MILITARY

TOGGLE COAT

DOUBLE-BREASTED

LADY COAT

LONG PEACOAT

RETRO STYLING

pick your favorites

WHITE-DENIM TRENCH

BELTED SUEDE

TRANSITIONAL COATS

VINTAGEY

SIDE-BUTTON

PIPED WOOL

PEACOAT

TAILORED

BLAZER STYLING

LIGHT WORK JACKETS

SIDE-BUTTON

DOUBLE-BREASTED

BELTED TWILL

BAND COLLAR

coats and clothes

SHEARLING

JEANS
+
HOBO BAG
+
ANKLE BOOTS

EVENING COAT

HANDKERCHIEF-HEM DRESS
+
LADY BAG
+
METALLIC SLINGBACKS

classic weekend look

the floaty hem peeks out beneath the coat

WINDBREAKER

CIRCLE SKIRT
+
RAFFIA TOTE
+
SPECTATOR SLINGBACKS

VINTAGE COAT

CHIFFON DRESS
+
EVENING BAG
+
KITTEN HEELS

an unexpected blend of sporty and feminine

reds work together when they're not part of an outfit

coats and clothes

PARKA

SHIFT
+
KNEE BOOTS
+
CUTOUT HANDBAG

BAND-COLLAR COAT

PENCIL SKIRT
+
KITTEN HEEL SLINGBACKS
+
STATUS BAG

cool juxtaposition of sporty and office-y

a neat-yet sexy-work ensemble

OVERCOAT

LITTLE BLACK DRESS
+
SEXY BOOTS
+
BUCKLE BAG

high-contrast and sleek

PEACOAT

MINISKIRT
+
FISHNETS
+
POINTY FLATS

perfectly proportioned pieces set off sexy legs

FASHION CHALLENGE:
accessorizing a coat

**PEACOAT
+
BUCKET HAT**

**PARKA
+
STRIPED CAP**

**SHEARLING
+
CROCHET FLOWER HAT**

clean lines,
head to hip

keeping it
casual

the
perfect shot
of femininity
and color

In winter, there's a fine line between cutting a dashing profile and looking like the crazy cat lady. The key is the chemistry between your coat and hat.

DOUBLE-BREASTED COAT
+
FUR TRAPPER

FAUX FUR JACKET
+
COLORBLOCK SKI CAP

OVERCOAT
+
NEWSBOY CAP

dress down a hyper-glam coat for daytime

a neutral coat allows for playfulness on top

balances the double-breasted seriousness

and you're back in sixth grade

A puffer coat can be sporty and cool, but with the wrong hat, it can make you look a tad unsophisticated. Skip the cutesy options and upgrade your look instead with a sleek hat with feminine details.

OTHER OPTIONS

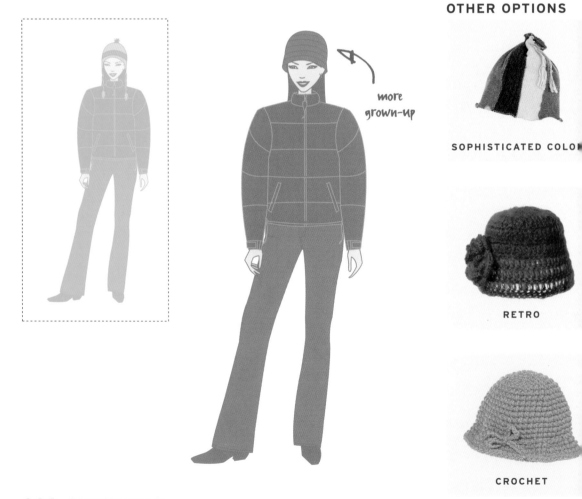

more grown-up

SOPHISTICATED COLOR

RETRO

CROCHET

IN THE FITTING ROOM

TRUST YOUR FIRST IMPRESSION

The right overcoat will look amazing the minute you slip it on—even if it needs some adjustments, like sleeve-shortening. If you look in the mirror and don't get that "wow" feeling, hang it up and move on.

BRING A SWEATER

When pre-season coat shopping, keep in mind that you'll be wearing heavier clothes come winter. Dress appropriately or bring along an extra layer so you can assess the true fit.

PUT YOUR HANDS IN THE AIR

An overcoat should be comfortable but tailored. The shoulders and underarms are the most critical fit points. If the sleeve is cut well and the coat fits up into the crook of your underarm, you should be able to lift your arms without the entire coat hiking up. Try it. If raising your hand yanks up the whole coat, it's not well cut and you should skip it.

LIGHTEN UP

With modern materials like Thinsulate, there's no need to be bulky to be warm. If you find yourself trying on puffy immobilizing parkas, maybe you're shopping in the wrong store. Try a fashion chain store or a catalogue rather than an outdoor-gear store (even if you insist on down). You can find sleeker shapes with better styling that may even make a casual coat office-appropriate.

spend or save?

There's no cheating here; a nice wool overcoat is going to cost you. Spend as much as you can afford because this purchase should carry you through at least five seasons. The place to save is on light spring outerwear—especially on fun, trendy pieces.

WHAT TO PACK FOR A THREE-DAY TRIP

The challenge of packing—no matter what length your trip—is to be prepared for multiple situations without bringing along everything you own. Whether you're leaving for three days or three weeks, you can travel light and still look great. All it takes is some simple packing policies.

1 **Pack things you love to wear.** A trip is no time to break in that sweater with the tags still on that you haven't found a single use for yet. If you don't wear it at home, you won't want to wear it away. Bring your favorite clothes, and you won't mind having less with you.

2 **Look at the big picture.** All the separates in your suitcase should combine well with each other—another argument for packing the things you wear most often. And always leave room for a purchase or two.

3 **Bring knit pieces rather than wovens;** they're wrinkle-resistant. Also, dark colors tend to look better upon a second-wear than light colors. And prints, though less versatile, hide wrinkles better than solids.

4 **Choose two thin items over one bulky one.** A chunky sweater takes up a huge amount of room in your travel bag, but two thin sweaters layer for just as much warmth and occupy a fraction of the real estate.

5 **Keep shoes down to a maximum of three pairs, no matter how long your trip;** that's two pairs in your luggage and one on your feet. This rule, brutal though it may seem, also forces you to think through potential outfits and carefully edit your choice of clothes.

... for a beach weekend

2 tanks

2 lightweight longsleeve tops

light dress

long summer pants

drawstring pants

2 swimsuits

pareo

big sun hat

light sweater

flat sandals

flip-flops

bangles

crushable beach bag

smaller straw bag

SEASIDE

BRUNCH

throw a top over it, and it's a skirt

SUNSET STROLL

... for a business trip

cute blazer

silky blouse

black sweater

beaded top

scoopneck tee

dark pants

jeans

pumps

ankle boots

pencil skirt

structured big bag

tiny bag for evening

trench

classic accessories

MEETING

WORKING DINNER

also great for meetings

OFF DUTY

... for a country getaway

tee

denim jacket

tank

western top

sweater

suede booties

hippie earrings

fringe bag

khakis

jeans

button-down

athletic shoe

NATURE WALK

ANTIQUING

BY THE FIRE

... for a city holiday

casual top

tank

neutral pants

beaded skirt

versatile skirt

evening top

heels

clutch

casual jacket

pencil skirt

flats

small tote

structured sweater

2 pairs of earrings

UPTOWN SHOPPING

THEATER NIGHT

SIGHTSEEING

a fabulous piece that packs easily

Lucky.

STREAMLINE YOUR WARDROBE

With what you now know, you're ready to evaluate your own closet and pare down. You may find yourself getting rid of more than you keep. But you'll be left with really functional pieces that show you at your best—and make it easy to get dressed in the morning.

getting started

1

Make sure you can see what you're doing. If your closet is overstuffed or otherwise hard to navigate, move everything onto the bed—along with the contents of relevant drawers.

2

Separate the front-runners. Grab your favorite pieces—those that make you look great—and put them back where they belong.

3

Toss worn-out stuff—items you've known for a long time should go—like hopelessly pilled sweaters, threadbare swimsuits, stained tees, and jeans torn beyond recognition.

4

Pull from the remaining pile those pieces in need of repair or alterations, with the plan of making one trip to the tailor for the lot.

Now it's time to start a giveaway bag (or two). If it's hard for you to part with your stuff, it sometimes helps to know where it's going. Once you find someone your size who actually wants your cast-offs, letting them go is a lot less difficult. Those pieces you're super-attached to can be eased out of your life in stages. Start by transferring them to a shopping bag in your closet. A week later, move them to another part of your home; next, leave them by the door. Pretty soon, you'll be glad to get rid of them.

what to keep, what to lose

Chances are, even after extracting the gold and tossing the garbage, the bulk of your wardrobe is still heaped on your bed. Now comes the hard part: evaluating—and saying good-bye to—much of your stuff.

Ask yourself the following questions about each item. A piece that gets yesses to all is a keeper. Everything else should probably go—including items that are all yesses but happen to reflect a long-dead and never-coming-back trend or those that, for no reason you can put your finger on, just don't work.

		YES	N
1	DOES IT FLATTER MY SHAPE?	○	○
2	IS THE FIT PERFECT OR FIXABLE?	○	○
3	IS THE COLOR RIGHT FOR ME?	○	○
4	HAVE I WORN IT IN THE LAST TWO YEARS?	○	○
5	DO I FEEL GREAT WHEN I WEAR IT?	○	○

There are a few reasons (beyond un-wearability) to save clothes. But anything you don't use regularly should be moved out of your bedroom closet into another space.

SENTIMENTAL REASONS

If we kept every item with a memory attached, we'd be buried in clothes. Consider possible reuse (concert tees versus, say, college sweatshirts), when drawing the line.

IT'S VERY VALUABLE

A vintage designer piece or a high-quality new purchase deserves some extra thought. If nothing else, holding onto it as an investment—with one eye on eBay—could make sense.

IT CAN SERVE ANOTHER PURPOSE

Tees that are too worn for work might be just fine for the gym. And the jeans you hemmed too short could be revived as cut-offs.

Hang onto high-quality shoes in good condition that aren't wildly trendy. Even if they're out of rotation for now, they could easily cycle back. Apply the same policy to accessories like belts and bags: Purge the trendy, inexpensive ones as soon as you can, but keep somewhat classic, well-made pieces for a future round. Store them away from your active wardrobe to minimize clutter.

tough calls: overcoming the urge to keep things you shouldn't

"PERFECT FIT, BUT NOT MY STYLE"
The dress you bought because it fit like it was custom-made—in spite of the weird embroidery on the neckline—remains unwearable because of said offensive detail. Change it or lose it.

"PERFECT STYLE, BUT DOESN'T FIT . . . YET"
Don't save a pair of jeans for that anticipated five-pound weight loss. Owning them is bad for your psyche. If the time comes when you drop a size, chances are you won't hesitate to run out and buy a new pair.

"PERFECT IN EVERY WAY . . . EXCEPT FOR THAT STAIN"
If it didn't come out at the cleaner's or as you toiled over it in the sink, it's permanent.

"THE NICEST THING I'VE EVER HAD"
There's a place for sentimental attachment and posterity. One cloth garment bag set aside to hold a couple of special items—maybe with the intention of one day passing them down—makes sense. Just be sure the bag doesn't start out full. And if there's anywhere else to put it, get it out of your closet.

"TOO EXPENSIVE TO THROW OUT"
If the piece doesn't work, look at it this way: You paid for it once in cash, and now you're paying for it again in valuable closet space. If it's not right for you, bite the bullet and let it go.

organizing your closet

BUY UNIFORM HANGERS	STORE SHOES IN CLEAR STACKING DRAWERS	INSTALL SHELF DIVIDERS	USE THE RIGHT TOOLS
A row of matching wooden hangers has amazing motivational effects. And when clothes hang neatly, they take up less space.	Choose drawers that are aerated—shoes need to breathe; an alternative is to keep shoes (labeled) on shelves in the boxes they came in.	Keep stacks of sweaters or jeans from toppling with shelf dividers. They can turn otherwise unusable high shelves into viable storage space.	A grid storage system makes it easy to put away belts and bags—and easy to see your options when getting dressed.

20 great pieces worth the expense

If there's any doubt where your wardrobe dollars are best spent, here are some surefire investments—pieces you can count on using for the next five years. When shopping for any of these items, spend a little more for a great fit or high-quality materials. You won't regret it.

cashmere sweater

parka

menswear trousers

trenchcoat

fitted blazer

overcoat

wool A-line skirt

fancy earrings

evening dress

black leather bag

black flats

black pumps

knee boots

leather jacket

sexy suit

strappy evening sandals

sequin top

sequin evening bag

good watch

leather tote

TAKING CARE OF YOUR CLOTHES

	HOW TO CLEAN	HOW TO STORE
cashmere or wool sweaters	Handwash in lukewarm water in delicate fabric wash. Roll in a towel to soak up excess water—never wring!—and dry flat.	Wrap loosely in white tissue paper, place in cloth bags, and seal with cedar chips to deter moths.
delicate tops (silk or cotton)	Dry-cleaning is usually preferred but some garments can be handwashed. Gently wash each item separately in lukewarm water and fabric wash. Hang dry.	Fold using white tissue paper, place in plastic bags with cedar chips, then stack in a storage box.
swimsuits, bras, and other lingerie	Handwash lingerie in lukewarm water in delicate fabric wash. Swimsuits should be hand-rinsed clean in cool water after each wearing.	Stack cups of bras and store in a not-too-crowded drawer.
jeans	Machine-wash jeans inside-out in cold water. To keep them looking new, handwash using cold water and delicate fabric wash.	Fold and stack. Hang your best pair if you use them for work.
suits and cloth coats	Dry-clean suits as infrequently as possible; it wears out the fabric. Dry-clean coats once a season.	In a cloth garment bag, never in dry-cleaner's plastic, which traps in chemicals.
leather and suede garments	Wipe leather clothes with a damp cloth and mild non-detergent soap, pat dry. Brush suedes with a bristle brush; light stains can be removed with a pencil eraser.	Hang in a well-ventilated closet; leather breathes and needs air circulation to prevent drying out.
shoes	Wipe leather shoes with a damp cloth and polish them regularly. Fix scuff marks with a cream polish one shade lighter than shoe color. For suedes, rub imperfections with a pencil eraser.	In the box the shoes came in, with holes poked through so air can circulate, or in aerated plastic bins.
boots	Wipe leather boots clean with a damp cloth and polish them regularly. If boots get wet outdoors, dry with a soft cloth rather than leaving them to air-dry; moisture can eventually damage leather.	In their own boxes, with cardboard boot shapers or stuffed with tissue paper to maintain the shape.
leather bags	For leather bags, wipe clean and use polish to touch up scuff marks. Silk or canvas bags should be professionally dry-cleaned.	Sit bags on a shelf. If you hang them by the handle, they can lose their shape.

10 LUCKY RULES OF SHOPPING

1 Always try it on, and always sit down in it.

2 Be sure you know the store's return policy.

3 If you're unsure about a big-ticket item, put it on hold for 24 hours and think it over.

4 Don't buy anything that doesn't flatter you or isn't comfortable, no matter how of-the-moment it is.

5 If you have to talk yourself into a purchase in the dressing room, pass on it.

6 In a shopping emergency, go for shapes or labels you know you can count on.

7 If there's nothing in your closet to wear with it, skip it.

8 Really amazing one-of-a-kind items will disappear; if you fall in love with one, buy it right away.

9 Never purchase something just because it looks good on someone else.

10 If you can't stop thinking about an item, go back and get it instantly.

shopping rules

SALE

1 Don't buy anything on sale that you wouldn't consider at full price.

2 Learn the markdown schedule at your favorite stores.

3 Shop sales on Friday nights, when no one else is there.

4 Use end-of-season sales to stock up on classics.

5 Befriend a salesperson; he or she might put sale items aside for you—or even give you markdowns before a sale officially begins.

VINTAGE

1 If a vintage item smells, don't buy it; chances are, it'll never come out.

2 Vintage shoes can be very narrow; be sure you can walk in them.

3 If you're shopping for serious estate jewelry, never purchase without having it assessed.

4 Look for woven (as opposed to printed) labels inside clothes, which can indicate better overall quality.

5 If fabric is threadbare, pass it up; there's no saving it.

DEPARTMENT STORE

1 Always check the boys department for sporty stuff— especially outerwear.

2 Try the juniors department for trendy items, at great prices.

3 Say yes to fake department store diamonds and pearls but no to fake silver and gold.

4 Most stores offer free alterations; take full advantage.

5 Know your rights: if an item is marked down soon after you buy it (usually up to two weeks after), you're entitled to a price adjustment.

COOL STORES AROUND THE COUNTRY

LABAMA

RMINGHAM
adora
21 18th St.
205-879-0335
s friendly shop mixes flirty and sleek
s by a wide range of designers.

RIZONA

AGSTAFF
falo Exchange
3 S. Plaza Way
928-556-0472
igner pieces and trendy items turn
at this hip secondhand chain.

HOENIX
falo Exchange
E. Missouri
602-532-0144
e Flagstaff, AZ, listing)

J's Designer Shoe Outlet
9 E. Camelback Rd., #2
602-234-0081
n high-end to more affordable
ads, the selection here
stantly changes.

OTTSDALE
J's Designer Shoe Outlet
6 E. Shea Blvd.
480-607-0170

51 N. Scottsdale Rd., Ste. 8A
480-609-6905
e Phoenix, AZ, listing)

ctric Ladyland
35 N. Scottsdale Rd.
480-948-9341
great boutique is full of
ted tees, patchwork items, and
ery baubles.

lvelvet
7 N. Scottsdale Rd.
ey Village
480-483-1760
nt on this store to provide the
st designs.

MPE
man Marcus Last Call
0 S. Arizona Mills Circle
ona Mills Mall
480-831-7979
man's clearinghouses stock
best lines at rock-bottom prices.

Off Fifth Saks Fifth Avenue
5000 Arizona Mills Circle
Arizona Mills Mall
Tel: 480-838-5708
With broad selection, current styles, and
great price reductions, this outlet is
one of the best.

TUCSON
Buffalo Exchange
2001 E. Speedway
Tel: 520-795-0508
and
6170 E. Speedway
Tel: 520-885-8392
(See Flagstaff, AZ, listing)

E & J's Designer Shoe Outlet
7401 N. La Cholla Blvd.
Tel: 520-498-1645
(See Phoenix, AZ, listing)

Tucson Thrift Shop &
The Other Side
319 and 321 N. Fourth Ave.
Tel: 520-623-8736
These sister stores have amazing vintage
clothing, accessories, and costumes.

W. Boutique
4340 N. Campbell Ave., Ste. 185
Tel: 520-577-3470
The selection includes pieces by Diane
von Furstenberg and Tom K. Nguyen.

ARKANSAS
LITTLE ROCK
Tulips
5817 Kavanaugh Blvd.
Tel: 501-614-7343
Casual, cute, and affordable styles are
the focus of this darling boutique.

CALIFORNIA
LOS ANGELES
American Rag
150 S. La Brea Ave.
Tel: 323-935-3154
Great local pieces accompany the
store's shoe, designer, and vintage sections.

Beige
7274 Beverly Blvd.
Tel: 323-549-0064
This boutique is aptly named for its
mostly earth-toned urban clothing.

Blonde
2430 Main St.
Santa Monica
Tel: 310-396-9113

This place is packed to its lofty ceilings
with labels you want right now.

Buffalo Exchange
131 N. La Brea Ave.
Tel: 323-938-8604
(See Flagstaff, AZ, listing)

Catwalk
459 N. Fairfax Ave.
Tel: 323-951-9255
The vintage designer clothing here—
Givenchy, YSL—is all in great condition.

Curve
154 N. Robertson Blvd.
Beverly Hills
Tel: 310-360-8008
This store sells adventurous pieces
from labels like Trosman Churba.

Debout Shoes
13023 Ventura Blvd.
Studio City
Tel: 818-906-7761
The mix of fashionable underground lab-
els at this shoe store makes it a hot spot.

Diavolina
334 S. La Brea Ave.
Tel: 323-936-5444
With its bold and showy selections, this
is our vote for the best L.A. shoe store.

Fred Segal
8100 Melrose Ave.
Tel: 323-651-4129
This store combines boutique intimacy
with department store–size inventory.

Fred Segal Flair
500 Broadway
Santa Monica
Tel: 310-451-7178
The racks of the up-to-the-millisecond
styles never feel picked over here.

Govinda's International Imports
3764 Watseka Ave.
Tel: 310-204-3263
This Hare Krishna–owned shop stocks
tons of embroidered cotton tops.

Hidden Treasures
154 S. Topanga Canyon Blvd.
Tel: 310-455-2998
This vintage shop sells linens, quilts, and
lots of whimsical secondhand finds.

Kitson
115 S. Robertson Blvd.
Tel: 310-859-2652
This shop's bags, belts, and jewelry
range from cute to sleek and sophisticated.

Last Chance
8712 Washington Blvd.
Culver City
Tel: 310-287-1919
The best deals on past- and current-
season designer goods are found here.

Lisa Kline
136 S. Robertson Blvd.
Tel: 310-246-0907
Swing by this store to pick up everything from dressy pieces to comfy tees.

Madison
9630 Brighton Way
Beverly Hills
Tel: 310-273-4787
This shop sells only highly desirable
shoes and accessories.

Oou
1764 N. Vermont Ave.
Tel: 323-665-6263
The name of the store will make perfect
sense once you see the clothing here.

Patty Faye
2910 Rowena Ave.
Tel: 323-667-1954
Items by Joie, Dessous Dessus, and
Beautiful People are housed in this space.

Sigerson Morrison
8307 W. Third St.
Tel: 323-655-6133
The dainty shoes with downtown
attitude inspire new-arrival frenzies.

Slow Clothing
7474 Melrose Ave.
Hollywood
Tel: 323-655-3725
Dominating a prime Melrose corner, this
cove of vintage wearables is fast
becoming a preferred destination.

Très Jolie LA
8327 Beverly Blvd.
Tel: 323-655-1110
This shop often beats out the
competition in carrying
up-and-coming labels.

The Wasteland
7428 Melrose Ave.
Tel: 323-653-3028
This popular secondhand spot is
packed with gently worn garments of
the designer variety.

Xin
8064 Melrose Ave.
Tel: 323-653-2188

COOL STORES AROUND THE COUNTRY 307
THE LUCKY SHOPPING MANUAL

ALABAMA

BIRMINGHAM

Theadora
2821 18th St.
Tel: 205-879-0335
This friendly shop mixes flirty and sleek looks by a wide range of designers.

ARIZONA

FLAGSTAFF

Buffalo Exchange
1113 S. Plaza Way
Tel: 928-556-0472
Designer pieces and trendy items turn up at this hip secondhand chain.

PHOENIX

Buffalo Exchange
730 E. Missouri
Tel: 602-532-0144
(See Flagstaff, AZ, listing)

E & J's Designer Shoe Outlet
1919 E. Camelback Rd., #2
Tel: 602-234-0081
From high-end to more affordable brands, the selection here constantly changes.

SCOTTSDALE

E & J's Designer Shoe Outlet
8666 E. Shea Blvd.
Tel: 480-607-0170
and
16251 N. Scottsdale Rd., Ste. 8A
Tel: 480-609-6905
(See Phoenix, AZ, listing)

Electric Ladyland
15435 N. Scottsdale Rd.
Tel: 480-948-9341
This great boutique is full of printed tees, patchwork items, and glittery baubles.

Redvelvet
8787 N. Scottsdale Rd.
Gainey Village
Tel: 480-483-1760
Count on this store to provide the latest designs.

TEMPE

Neiman Marcus Last Call
5000 S. Arizona Mills Circle
Arizona Mills Mall
Tel: 480-831-7979
Neiman's clearinghouses stock the best lines at rock-bottom prices.

Off Fifth Saks Fifth Avenue
5000 Arizona Mills Circle
Arizona Mills Mall
Tel: 480-838-5708
With broad selection, current styles, and great price reductions, this outlet is
one of the best.

TUCSON

Buffalo Exchange
2001 E. Speedway
Tel: 520-795-0508
and
6170 E. Speedway
Tel: 520-885-8392
(See Flagstaff, AZ, listing)

E & J's Designer Shoe Outlet
7401 N. La Cholla Blvd.
Tel: 520-498-1645
(See Phoenix, AZ, listing)

Tucson Thrift Shop & The Other Side
319 and 321 N. Fourth Ave.
Tel: 520-623-8736
These sister stores have amazing vintage clothing, accessories, and costumes.

W. Boutique
4340 N. Campbell Ave., Ste. 185
Tel: 520-577-3470
The selection includes pieces by Diane von Furstenberg and Tom K. Nguyen.

ARKANSAS

LITTLE ROCK

Tulips
5817 Kavanaugh Blvd.
Tel: 501-614-7343
Casual, cute, and affordable styles are the focus of this darling boutique.

CALIFORNIA

LOS ANGELES

American Rag
150 S. La Brea Ave.
Tel: 323-935-3154
Great local pieces accompany the store's shoe, designer, and vintage sections.

Beige
7274 Beverly Blvd.
Tel: 323-549-0064
This boutique is aptly named for its mostly earth-toned urban clothing.

Blonde
2430 Main St.
Santa Monica
Tel: 310-396-9113
This place is packed to its lofty ceilings with labels you want right now.

Buffalo Exchange
131 N. La Brea Ave.
Tel: 323-938-8604
(See Flagstaff, AZ, listing)

Catwalk
459 N. Fairfax Ave.
Tel: 323-951-9255
The vintage designer clothing here—Givenchy, YSL—is all in great condition.

Curve
154 N. Robertson Blvd.
Beverly Hills
Tel: 310-360-8008
This store sells adventurous pieces from labels like Trosman Churba.

Debout Shoes
13023 Ventura Blvd.
Studio City
Tel: 818-906-7761
The mix of fashionable underground labels at this shoe store makes it a hot spot.

Diavolina
334 S. La Brea Ave.
Tel: 323-936-5444
With its bold and showy selections, this is our vote for the best L.A. shoe store.

Fred Segal
8100 Melrose Ave.
Tel: 323-651-4129
This store combines boutique intimacy with department store–size inventory.

Fred Segal Flair
500 Broadway
Santa Monica
Tel: 310-451-7178
The racks of the up-to-the-millisecond styles never feel picked over here.

Govinda's International Imports
3764 Watseka Ave.
Tel: 310-204-3263
This Hare Krishna–owned shop stocks tons of embroidered cotton tops.

Hidden Treasures
154 S. Topanga Canyon Blvd.
Tel: 310-455-2998
This vintage shop sells linens, quilts, and lots of whimsical secondhand finds.

Kitson
115 S. Robertson Blvd.
Tel: 310-859-2652
This shop's bags, belts, and jewelry range from cute to sleek and sophisticated.

Last Chance
8712 Washington Blvd.
Culver City
Tel: 310-287-1919
The best deals on past- and current-season designer goods are found here.

Lisa Kline
136 S. Robertson Blvd.
Tel: 310-246-0907
Swing by this store to pick up everything from dressy pieces to comfy tees.

Madison
9630 Brighton Way
Beverly Hills
Tel: 310-273-4787
This shop sells only highly desirable shoes and accessories.

Oou
1764 N. Vermont Ave.
Tel: 310-665-6263
The name of the store will make perfect sense once you see the clothing here.

Patty Faye
2910 Rowena Ave.
Tel: 323-667-1954
Items by Joie, DessousDessus, and Beautiful People are housed in this space.

Sigerson Morrison
8307 W. Third St.
Tel: 323-655-6133
The dainty shoes with downtown attitude inspire new-arrival frenzies.

Slow Clothing
7474 Melrose Ave.
Hollywood
Tel: 323-655-3725
Dominating a prime Melrose corner, this cove of vintage wearables is fast becoming a preferred destination.

Très Jolie LA

Locals stay true to the well-edited clothing at this neighborhood boutique.

Sunhee Moon
142 Fillmore St.
Tel: 415-355-1800
This local designer sells kimono tops and sweet boatnecks.

The Bar
340 Presidio Blvd.
Tel: 415-409-4901
The garments are as clean and crisp as the gloriously minimal shop.

The Wasteland
1660 Haight St.
Tel: 415-863-3150
San Francisco's best vintage store, with items from the '60s to the '80s.

Twenty Two
5856 College Ave.
Oakland
Tel: 510-594-2201
The shoe collection juxtaposes special-edition sneakers with upscale lines.

Twenty-Six
1219 Main St.
St. Helena
Tel: 707-963-0495
This store is filled with tops, accessories, and varieties of hot denim brands.

Ver Unica
2378 Hayes St.
Tel: 415-431-0688
This vintage apparel and accessories shop stands out for its selectivity.

COLORADO
DENVER
Ace Dry Goods
78 S. Broadway
Tel: 303-733-2237
This retro store stocks everything from swing shoes to vintage belt buckles.

brandis b.
218 Steele St.
Tel: 303-333-4733
This boutique stocks distinctive denim and statement-making accessories.

Buffalo Exchange
230 E. 13th Ave.
Tel: 303-866-0165
and

1717 Walnut St.
Boulder
Tel: 303-938-1924
(See Flagstaff, AZ, listing)

Cry Baby Ranch
1422 Larimer St.
Tel: 303-623-3979
Come here for colorful cowgirl boots and vintage reproduction Western shirts.

Decade
56 S. Broadway
Tel: 303-733-2288
This store is filled with mostly new (though vintage-feeling) clothing.

Mariel
1420 Larimer St.
Tel: 303-623-1151
Find looks made of velvet and lace at this modern Victorian boutique.

MAX
3039 E. Third Ave.
Tel: 303-321-4949
You'll find great pieces at this store, which is always ahead of the style curve.

Miss Talulah's
1311 22nd St.
Tel: 303-293-8436
This tiny boutique in the shadow of Coors Field is a trove of pretty fashions.

MOD Livin'
5327 E. Colfax Ave.
Tel: 720-941-9292
This vintage emporium has just about anything from the '20s to the '70s.

Neiman Marcus Last Call
14500 W. Colfax Ave., #241
Lakewood
Tel: 303-273-5440
(See Tempe, AZ, listing)

Sunneshine Couture
3003 E. Third Ave.
Tel: 303-393-7414
This cool indie shop stocks hard-to-find denim and locally designed accessories.

CONNECTICUT
GREENWICH
Saturnia
39 Lewis St.
Tel: 203-625-0390

This shop is aimed at women who are looking for fun styles with lots of color.

Saturnia Blue
60 Lewis St.
Tel: 203-618-1904
Saturnia's sister store specializes in jeans and tees.

DISTRICT OF COLUMBIA
All About Jane
2438½ 18th St. N.W.
Tel: 202-797-9710
This store consistently stocks well-chosen, broad-appeal items like basic tees, a neat-fitting skirt, and the latest jeans.

Daisy Too
1814 Adams Mill Rd.
Tel: 202-797-1777
Come here for Rebecca Taylor, Jill Stuart, and an entire room of sales.

Kaur
2102 18th St. N.W.
Tel: 202-299-0404
Color is key at this shop, which has a load of printed garments.

Meeps & Aunt Neensie's Fashionette
1520 U St. N.W.
Tel: 202-265-6546
A wealth of '70s-inspired pieces and collectibles will make vintage clothing lovers go nuts.

FLORIDA
BOCA RATON
A Nose for Clothes
21306 St. Andrews Blvd.
Tel: 561-368-4602
You'll find everything from Michael Stars tees to Trina Turk palazzo pants here.

CORAL SPRINGS
A Nose for Clothes
1315 N. University Dr.
Tel: 954-753-0202
(See Boca Raton, FL, listing)

HOLLYWOOD
A Nose for Clothes
3359 Sheridan St.
Tel: 954-963-0030
(See Boca Raton, FL, listing)

MIAMI
A Nose for Clothes
2830 N.E. 187th St.
Aventura
Tel: 305-935-1022
and
11223 S. Dixie Highway
Pinecrest
Tel: 305-253-8632
(See Boca Raton, FL, listing)

Chroma
920 Lincoln Rd.
Miami Beach
Tel: 305-695-8808
The minimal space houses merchandise splashed in dozens of shades and prints.

En Avance
734 Lincoln Rd.
Tel: 305-534-0337
Find the latest looks, from Juicy Couture to Rebecca Taylor, at this trendy spot.

Intermix
634 Collins Ave.
Miami Beach
Tel: 305-531-5950
This chain is known for carrying a well-rounded selection of the best designers.

Lisa's Boutique
5845 Sunset Dr.
Tel: 305-669-8389
Hip labels like Hard Tail, Theory, Only Hearts, and William B. are carried here.

Neiman Marcus Last Call
12801 West Sunrise Blvd.
Fort Lauderdale
Tel: 954-846-9777
(See Tempe, AZ, listing)

Scoop
1901 Collins Ave.
Tel: 305-532-5929
This boutique chain has the best pieces from the best lines at any given moment.

Steam on Sunset
5830 Sunset Dr.
Tel: 305-669-9991
There are always great pieces by Project Alabama and Jiwon Park at this shop.

Tupelo Honey
8888 S.W. 136th St.
Tel: 305-235-9700
and
3585 N.E. 207th St., #5B
Tel: 305-936-9300
If you're after great jeans, stop by for Diesel, Lucky, Earl, Seven, and more.

ORLANDO
Zou Zou
2 N. Summerlin Ave.
Tel: 407-843-3373
This gem of a boutique stocks favorite feminine brands plus fun accessories.

PLANTATION
A Nose for Clothes
835 N. Nob Hill Rd.
Tel: 954-382-1080
(See Boca Raton, FL, listing)

WEST PALM BEACH
A Nose for Clothes
477 S. Rosemary Ave.
Tel: 561-832-3683
(See Boca Raton, FL, listing)

GEORGIA
ATHENS
Encore
186 E. Clayton St.
Tel: 706-354-8826
It's the only place for miles to get the latest jeans and tees, plus sweet dresses, tops, and shoes.

ATLANTA
A Nose for Clothes
4920 Roswell Rd. N.E.
Tel: 404-255-5756
and
9700 Medlock Bridge Rd.
Duluth
Tel: 678-473-0828
(See Boca Raton, FL, listing)

Blue Genes
3400 Around Lenox Rd. N.E.
Ste. 214
Tel: 404-231-3400
The best denim-heavy shop, with an extensive mix of designer goodies.

Bob Ellis Shoes
Phipps Plaza
3500 Peachtree Rd. N.E.
Tel: 404-841-0215
A stellar selection make this a top footwear and accessories boutique.

Fem Deluxe
2770 Lenox Rd. N.E.
Tel: 404-995-0299
A sexy boutique filled with Roberto Cavalli, Giuseppe Zanotti, and House of Field brands.

KLA
3400 Wooddale Dr. N.E.
Tel: 404-848-1414
The superlow jeans, slinky dresses, and separates handpicked from Brazil are racy but curve-friendly too.

L'Asia
2985 N. Fulton Dr. N.E.
Tel: 404-264-1222
Come here for bold footwear such as fur-trimmed boots and metallic-colored mules.

Luna
3167 Peachtree Rd. N.E.
Tel: 404-233-5344
This chainlet caters to women who favor trendy wearables with a ladylike slant.

Market
2770 Lenox Rd.
Tel: 404-814-0977
This creatively themed boutique makes it a mission to constantly update the roster of labels.

Mitzi & Romano
1038 N. Highland Ave. N.E.
Tel: 404-876-7228
A fresh, feminine vibe infuses this destination with hip yet affordable apparel.

Neiman Marcus Last Call
5900 Sugarloaf Parkway
Lawrenceville
Tel: 678-847-5777
(See Tempe, AZ, listing)

Sage
37 W. Paces Ferry Rd. N.W.
Tel: 404-233-8280
and
1745 Peachtree St. N.E., #L
Tel: 404-815-0555
Pick up sexy tops, body-conscious dresses, and cute silver jewelry here.

Scout
1198 Howell Mill Rd. N.W., Ste. 114
Tel: 404-605-0900
This serene space is home to many labels unavailable in the rest of the city.

T. Women's Clothing Etc.
9700 Medlock Bridge Rd., Ste. 117
Duluth
Tel: 678-957-1292
One of Atlanta's most extensively stocked boutiques.

HAWAII
Adasa
25 Maluniu Ave.
Kailua
Tel: 808-263-8500
This has clothing finds you'd expect in only the most urbane cities.

Aloha Rag
1221 Kapiolani Blvd.
Honolulu
Tel: 808-589-1352
Expect ultratrendy items at this airy boutique.

eden
75-5660 Kopiko St., #B5
Kailua Kona
Tel: 808-331-2776
The merchandise at this cheery boutique is feminine without veering into nauseatingly cute territory.

IDAHO
BOISE
Buffalo Exchange
1467 Milwaukee
Tel: 208-373-7714
(See Flagstaff, AZ, listing)

ILLINOIS
CHICAGO
Active Endeavors
935 W. Armitage Ave.
Tel: 773-281-8100
and
55 E. Grand Ave.
Tel: 312-822-0600
Hip high-performance clothing coexists with less sporty but still hot labels.

Flashy Trash
3524 N. Halsted St.
Tel: 773-327-6900
This vintage shop has one of the greatest retro stashes around.

Josephine
1405 N. Wells St.
Tel: 312-274-0359

The incredible selection at this shoe boutique features the highest-end brands.

Krista K
3458 N. Southport Ave.
Tel: 773-248-1967
This place is stocked with a slew of denim by emerging lines and great office-to-cocktails essentials.

Lori's Designer Shoes
824 W. Armitage Ave.
Tel: 773-281-5655
Slightly discounted, the latest and greatest hot lines are sold here.

Marshall Field's
111 N. State St.
Tel: 312-781-1000
Great basics can be found at every price point at this flagship store, but the real draw is the couture department—the largest in the city, with goods marked down as much as 80 percent each season.

p.45
1643 N. Damen Ave.
Tel: 773-862-4523
A cadre of up-and-coming designers with the edgiest trends.

Penelope's
1913 W. Division St.
Tel: 773-395-2351
Zero-attitude shopping with a great selection of clothing.

Public I
1923 W. Division St.
Tel: 773-772-9088
This shop offers variety with broad appeal, and hosts regular in-store events.

Red Head
3450 N. Southport Ave.
Tel: 773-325-9898
Find sweetly feminine clothing in this parlourlike boutique.

Robin Richman
2108 N. Damen Ave.
Tel: 773-278-6150
This clothing and accessory boutique carries many handmade items by local designers or imported from Europe.

Shopgirl
1206 W. Webster Ave.
Tel: 773-935-7467

Come here for suits with details, flirty dresses, and a nice array of tees and jeans.

Smack
1650 W. Division St.
Tel: 773-227-2008
Faux-flower garlands and pots of bright blooms fill this boutique of insider favorites.

Sugar Magnolia
34 E. Oak St.
Tel: 312-944-0885
The exuberance of the '70s meets the choicest trends of today.

Tangerine
1719 N. Damen Ave.
Tel: 773-772-0505
This boutique carries both a large volume and a wide array of appealing lines.

LOUISIANA
NEW ORLEANS
Angelique
7725 Maple St.
Tel: 504-866-1092
The antithesis of the overly trendy boutiques, this shop carries an ample selection of fashion-editor-favored labels.

Hemline
609 Chartres St.
Tel: 504-529-3566
and
838 Royal St.
Tel: 504-522-8577
and
3025 Magazine St.
Tel: 504-269-4005
and
7916 Maple St.
Tel: 504-862-0420
This string of boutiques mixes up-to-the-microsecond labels with established names.

Pied Nu
5521 Magazine St.
Tel: 504-899-4118
The back of this varied clothing and housewares emporium is dedicated to labels like Martin, Mayle, and Sigerson Morrison.

Victoria's Designer Shoes
7725 Maple St.
Tel: 504-861-8861
and

532 Chartres St.
Tel: 504-568-9990
Serious shoe collectors will appreciate the range of labels here.

MARYLAND
BALTIMORE
Cherry Tomato Boutique
815 N. Charles St.
Tel: 410-332-9917
Lines that are hard to come by in D.C. are easy to find at this boutique.

Shine
3554 Roland Ave.
Tel: 410-366-6100
Open only from Thursday to Sunday, this boutique stocks finds like studded nylon duffel bags.

MASSACHUSETTS
BOSTON
Eye of the Needle
85 Newbury St.
Tel: 617-859-7999
This shop's a reliable source of weekend-at-the-beach essentials.

Filene's Basement
426 Washington St.
Tel: 617-542-2011
An old-school bargain palace.

Gretta Luxe
94 Central St.
Wellesley
Tel: 781-237-7010
From spa roots, this boutique has come to stock clothing by Chloé, Marc by Marc Jacobs, and Jimmy Choo shoes.

Intermix
186 Newbury St.
Tel: 617-236-5172
(See Miami, FL, listing.)

Jasmine Sola
344 Newbury St.
Tel: 617-867-4630
and
37 Brattle St.
Cambridge
Tel: 617-354-6043
and
1760 Massachusetts Ave.
Cambridge
Tel: 617-576-0806
and

199 Boylston St.
Newton
Tel: 617-332-8415
This chain of emporiums purveys the ultimate American uniform with a funky edge.

Louis Boston
234 Berkeley St.
Tel: 617-262-6100
The best all-around shopping destination in Boston.

MAP
623 Tremont St.
Tel: 617-247-6230
Clothing and accessories for women join the male fare here.

Moxie
73 Charles St. 1A
Tel: 617-557-9991
This shoe boutique offers both safe and boundary-expanding styles.

Native Sun
365 Boston Post Rd.
Sudbury
Tel: 978-440-7854
Steer clear of Boston's busy bustle while stocking up on prime brands.

The Garment District
200 Broadway
Cambridge
Tel: 617-876-5230
This warehouse-size secondhand shop boasts a 100,000-piece inventory.

Wish
49 Charles St.
Tel: 617-227-4441
Friendly fashion advice is offered at this packed neighborhood shop.

MICHIGAN
DETROIT
Caruso, Caruso
193 W. Maple Rd.
Birmingham
Tel: 248-645-5151
This urban contemporary shop stocks brands for a hip weekend wardrobe.

Edward Dorian
237 Pierce St.
Birmingham
Tel: 248-642-9424
Clothes by Vivienne Tam and Poleci are the main draw at this trendy boutique.

Imelda's Closet
123 W. Maple Rd.
Birmingham
Tel: 248-203-1222
Detroit's best shoes can be found at this super-sleek boutique.

Mark Keller
130a W. Maple Rd.
Birmingham
Tel: 248-258-5454
An old horse barn houses sweet tees, dresses, knits, and mules.

Neiman Marcus Last Call
4030 Baldwin Rd.
Auburn Hills
Tel: 248-745-6868
(See Tempe, AZ, listing)

Ripe
1444 Lake Dr. S.E.
Grand Rapids
Tel: 616-458-4113
and
217 S. Kalamazoo Mall
Kalamazoo
Tel: 269-343-6336
Pick up sexy pencil skirts, tailored tees, and funky bright tennis shoes here.

TENDER
271 W. Maple Rd.
Birmingham
Tel: 248-258-0212
The best designer clothes are offered here in a no-attitude environment.

Vain Couture
340 S. Main St.
Royal Oak
Tel: 248-546-0900
This eclectic boutique showcases young designers on their way up.

Vintagey
141 E. Front St.
Traverse City
Tel: 231-933-4207
This vintage shop is completely dedicated to '60s and '70s wearables.

MONTANA
BOZEMAN
Buffalo Exchange
1005 W. Main
Tel: 406-585-9952
(See Flagstaff, AZ, listing.)

NEVADA
LAS VEGAS
Buffalo Exchange
4110 S. Maryland Parkway
Tel: 702-791-3960
(See Flagstaff, AZ, listing)

Musette
The Village Square Shopping Center
9420 W. Sahara Ave.
Ft. Apache at Sahara
Tel: 702-309-6873
This minimalist boutique has a phe-
nomenal selection, specifically of
denim, with a highlight on up-and-
coming brands.

PRIMM
Neiman Marcus Last Call
32100 S. Las Vegas Blvd.
Tel: 702-874-2100
(See Tempe, AZ, listing)

NEW JERSEY
ELIZABETH
Neiman Marcus Last Call
651 Kapkowski Rd.
Tel: 908-994-1911
(See Tempe, AZ, listing)

MOUNT LAUREL
Shop
1203 Rte. 73 N.
Tel: 856-787-0330
This boutique draws locals in droves
with its perfect balance of wild and
mellow clothing.

NEW MEXICO
ALBUQUERQUE
Buffalo Exchange
3005 Central Ave. N.E.
Tel: 505-262-0098
(See Flagstaff, AZ, listing)

Elsa Ross
3511 Central Ave. N.E.
Tel: 505-265-2070
This longstanding favorite
carries lines like Seven, Juicy,
and Development.

Ruby Shoesday
228 Gold Ave. S.W.
Tel: 505-848-7829
The lively local owner presents labels
such as Camper and Lulu Guinness.

SANTA FE
Bodhi Bazaar
500 Montezuma Ave., Sanbusco
Market Center
Tel: 505-982-3880
The hippie wear of the past has been
replaced by a stellar selection of
wearables by trendy lines.

NEW YORK
CENTRAL VALLEY
Neiman Marcus Last Call
934 Grapevine Ct.
Tel: 845-928-4978
(See Tempe, AZ, listing)

**Woodbury Common
Premium Outlets**
Tel: 845-928-4000
The country's best outlet mall, hands
down—all the designers are there.

NEW YORK CITY
Anna
150 E. 3rd St.
Tel: 212-358-0195
This cute store mixes the owner
Kathy Kemp's own line with select
vintage and local designers.

Barneys New York
660 Madison Ave.
Tel: 212-826-8900
New York City's best
department store, known for
its great shoe department.

Barneys Co-op
236 W. 18th St.
Tel: 212-593-7800
and
116 Wooster St.
Tel: 212-965-9964
Downtown girls access the beyond-
hip Barneys wares here without the
uptown schlep.

Butter
407 Atlantic Ave.
Brooklyn
Tel: 718-260-9033
Owner Eva Weiss stocks the
absolute best and newest indie
designers out there. A *Lucky*
favorite.

Cantaloup
1036 Lexington Ave.
Tel: 212-249-3566

Century 21
22 Cortlandt St.
Tel: 212-227-9092
This gigantic designer discount
department store has amazing deals
on nearly every big name.

Diane T.
174 Court St.
Brooklyn
Tel: 718-923-5777
This shop carries lines like
Longchamp, Rebecca Taylor, and
Paul & Joe.

DKNY
655 Madison Ave.
Tel: 212-223-3569
and
420 West Broadway
Tel: 646-613-1100
Each shop is architecturally magnifi-
cent, combining gifts, accessories,
and clothing.

Find Outlet
361 W. 17th St.
Tel: 212-243-3177
Restocked weekly, current-season
small designer items sell here for half
off and more.

Foley + Corinna
108 Stanton St.
Tel: 212-529-2338
This boutique's clothing is half
vintage, half original.

Geraldine
246 Mott St.
Tel: 212-219-1620
Tastefully radical shoes line the
shelves of this tiny Nolita shop.

Henri Bendel
712 Fifth Ave.
Tel: 212-247-1100
The indie department store known
for taking chances on new designers.

Hollywould
198 Elizabeth St.
Tel: 212-343-8344
Holly's shoes combine color with cute
leather flowers, pattern, and sexy-
yet-pretty stilettos.

Intermix
1003 Madison Ave.
Tel: 212-249-7858
and
125 Fifth Ave.
Tel: 212-533-9720
and

210 Columbus Ave.
Tel: 212-769-9116
(See Miami, FL, listing)

Isa
88 N. 6th St.
Brooklyn
Tel: 718-387-3363
One of Williamsburg's retail pioneers,
this arty shop sells experimental
clothing in a lofty space.

Jeffrey
449 W. 14th St.
Tel: 212-206-1272
Larger than a boutique, smaller than
a department store, and known for a
great shoe selection.

Jim Smiley Vintage Clothing
128 W. 23rd St.
Tel: 212-741-1195
Excellent-condition clothing from
the turn of the century forward,
and impossible-to-find vintage
designer pieces.

Kirna Zabete
96 Greene St.
Tel: 212-941-9656
This avant-garde boutique boasts
an incredible mix of labels and
gorgeous merchandising.

Language
238 Mulberry St.
Tel: 212-431-5566
DJs, filmmakers, and artists favor
the funky mix of this fashion and
furniture destination.

Marc Jacobs
163 Mercer St.
Tel: 212-343-1490
Anyone in search of Jacobs's great
coats and super-flattering jeans
must stop by his chic SoHo boutique.

Martin
206 E. 6th St.
Tel: 212-358-0011
Photos of style icons line the brick
walls here, evident inspiration for the
tops, jackets, and perfectly hip-
hugging jeans.

Otte
218 Bedford Ave.
Brooklyn
Tel: 718-302-3007
and
121 Greenwich Ave.
Tel: 212-229-9424

Clothing and accessories here are girlish and sexy-hip.

Otto Tootsi Plohound
273 Lafayette St.
Tel: 212-431-7299
and
413 West Broadway
Tel: 212-925-8931
and
137 Fifth Ave.
Tel: 212-460-8650
and
38 E. 57th St.
Tel: 212-231-3199
Adventurous shoe-lovers come here for a broad selection of nonconformist lines.

Patch NYC
17 Eighth Ave.
Tel: 212-807-1060
This handbag line is known for its arts-and-crafts feel.

Pearl River Mart
477 Broadway
Tel: 212-431-7388
This Chinese department store is filled with imports like beaded slippers, silk purses, and jackets.

Rafé
1 Bleeker St.
Tel: 212-780-9739
This wide-appeal accessory line often uses graphic printed fabric.

Scoop
1275 Third Ave.
Tel: 212-535-5577
and
532 Broadway
Tel: 212-925-2886
(See Miami, FL, listing)

Shop
105 Stanton St.
Tel: 212-375-0304
The epicenter of Lower East Side coolness, this small store has the best roster of the newest small designers.

Sigerson Morrison
28 Prince St.
Tel: 212-219-3893
(See Los Angeles, CA, listing)

SSS Sample Sales
261 W. 36th St.
Tel: 212-947-8748
Label junkies brave long lines at this warehouse to score current-season designer stock.

Steven Alan
103 Franklin St.
Tel: 212-343-0692
The second location of this priority shopping stop carries an even greater quantity of hard-to-find labels.

TG170
170 Ludlow St.
Tel: 212-995-8660
The first boutique to open on the Lower East Side, it's still ahead of the trends.

OHIO
COLUMBUS
Principessa
1257 Grandview Ave.
Grandview Heights
Tel: 614-488-2080
Young career women and university students alike favor this bubblegum-hued boutique.

OREGON
EUGENE
Buffalo Exchange
131 E. Fifth Ave.
Tel: 541-687-2805
(See Flagstaff, AZ, listing)

PORTLAND
Buffalo Exchange
1420 S.E. 37th Ave.
Tel: 503-234-1302
and
1036 W. Burnside
Tel: 503-222-3418
(See Flagstaff, AZ, listing)

Magpie
520 S.W. Ninth Ave.
Tel: 503-220-0920
This spic-and-span vintage shop organizes racks first by decade, then by color.

Odessa
718 N.W. 11th Ave.
Tel: 503-223-1998
Our favorite Oregon shopping destination, with a deft mix of national labels and local designs.

Pokerface
128 S.W. Third Ave.
Tel: 503-294-0445

The astounding range of labels at this ballroom-size shop could easily rival that of a New York or a London boutique.

Red Light Clothing Exchange
3590 S.E. Hawthorne Blvd.
Tel: 503-963-8888
Our favorite of Portland's many vintage stores, this one has reasonable prices and large volume.

PENNSYLVANIA
PHILADELPHIA
Adresse
1706 Locust St.
Tel: 215-985-3161
This boutique features favorites such as Katayone Adeli and Paul Smith.

Buffalo Exchange
1109 Walnut St.
Tel: 215-627-4647
(See Flagstaff, AZ, listing)

Claire Dickson Boutique
545 Germantown Pike
Lafayette Hill
Tel: 610-825-8668
Feminine and comfortable, this store sells classics and the latest upscale looks.

Joan Shepp
1616 Walnut St.
Tel: 215-735-2666
The high fashion here is never conservative and always interesting.

Knit Wit
1718 Walnut St.
Tel: 215-564-4760
Both longstanding and fresh, filled with an inventory of the latest names.

Neiman Marcus Last Call
1634 Franklin Mills Circle
Tel: 215-637-5900
(See Tempe, AZ, listing)

Petulia's Folly
1710 Sansom St.
Tel: 215-569-1344
This shop's monumental array of hard-to-find goods includes slim pants, slinky tops, and hand-dyed scarves.

Skirt
907 W. Lancaster Ave.
Bryn Mawr
Tel: 610-520-0222

A great selection of thoroughly feminine clothing by the likes of Nanette Lepore and Tocca—and lots of skirts.

Vagabond
37 N. Third St.
Tel: 267-671-0737
This Old City boutique carries cutting-edge brands and original pieces by local designers (including the owners).

PUERTO RICO
SAN JUAN
Ego
318 Ave. F. D. Roosevelt
Tel: 787-781-8670
An entire vacation wardrobe can be scored in one visit at this packed shop.

Oui
348 Ave. F. D. Roosevelt
Tel: 787-765-2424
This tri-level wonder sits on our top-10 list of all-time best boutiques; the shoe salon and the expanded clothing selection are both exceptional.

SOUTH CAROLINA
CHARLESTON
Bob Ellis Shoes
332 King St.
Tel: 843-723-2945
This shop has an amazing selection of the very best designer shoes.

TENNESEE
NASHVILLE
Jamie Inc.
4317 Harding Pike
Tel: 615-292-4188
A local fashion institution, this is where Nashville women go to splurge.

TEXAS
AUSTIN
Buffalo Exchange
2904 Guadalupe St.
Tel: 512-480-9922
(See Flagstaff, AZ, listing)

By George
524 N. Lamar Blvd., #103
Tel: 512-472-5951

This understated clothing boutique offers Austin's best-edited selection of labels.

Neiman Marcus Last Call
4115 S. Capital of Texas Highway
Tel: 512-447-0701
(See Tempe, AZ, listing)

Shiki
3407H Guadalupe St.
Tel: 512-371-7767
Hard-to-find upstart designer labels are the specialty here.

Therapy
1113 S. Congress Ave.
Tel: 512-326-2331
Local women buck the laid-back trend for the occasional designer label here.

DALLAS
Buffalo Exchange
3424 Greenville
Tel: 214-826-7544
(See Flagstaff, AZ, listing)

Elements
4400 Lovers Lane
Tel: 214-987-0837
In addition to its exciting choice of clothing by Roberto Cavalli, Moschino, and Dolce & Gabbana, this boutique carries lingerie and sandals.

Forty Five Ten
4510 McKinney Ave.
Tel: 214-559-4510
The selection of both classic and trend-forward designer pieces is unparalleled in the region.

Jean Connection
5926 W. Northwest Highway
Tel: 214-691-7894
There's a denim style in stock for almost every size and shape here.

Movida
5321 E. Mockingbird Ln., Ste. 130
Tel: 214-821-8669
Ethnic-inspired trends mix with preppy sweaters and chunky jewelry at this must-go shop.

Neiman Marcus
1618 Main St.
Tel: 214-741-6911
The flagship of this designer department store opened in 1907.

Neiman Marcus Last Call
3000 Grapevine Mills Parkway #233
Grapevine
Tel: 214-513-1527
(See Tempe, AZ, listing)

Spicy Couture
5600 W. Lovers Lane, Ste. 143
Tel: 214-357-6555
This shop has developed a name for carrying unique, statement-making separates, shoes, jewelry, and other accessories.

HOUSTON
Buffalo Exchange
1614 Westheimer Rd.
Tel: 713-523-8701
(See Flagstaff, AZ, listing)

Miel de Abejas
2815 Westheimer Rd.
Tel: 713-522-3025
This chic shop is filled with styles from Milly, Petit Bateau, and Cosabella.

mix
2818 Kirby Dr.
Tel: 713-522-0606
A stellar collection of Balenciaga, Helmut Lang, Mayle, and more is available here.

Sloan/Hall
2620 Westheimer
Tel: 713-942-0202
You'll find a sophisticated and well-edited selection of clothing and jewelry among the housewares and beauty products.

Velvet Slipper
1151-10 Uptown Park Blvd.
Tel: 713-850-9828
This Venice-meets-Texas-decorated shoe boutique stocks exceptionally pretty heels.

UTAH
PARK CITY
Chloe Lane
556 Main St.
Tel: 435-645-9888
Filled with accessories, clothing, sleepwear, and other essentials, this shop aims to be a one-stop destination.

VIRGINIA
ARLINGTON
What's In
1101 S. Joyce St., Ste. B6
Tel: 703-414-3353
This front-runner for favorite D.C.-area boutique carries a vast array of dresses, swimwear, jeans, sexy mules, and delicate jewelry.

WASHINGTON
SEATTLE
Alhambra
101 Pine St.
Tel: 206-621-9571
One-of-a-kind Turkish pieces, hats by local milliners, and loads of silver jewelry with semiprecious stones can be found here.

Atlas Clothing Co.
1515 Broadway
Tel: 206-323-0960
Well-organized and cherry-picked vintage clothing, including jeans from the '70s through the '90s.

Bliss
3501 Fremont Ave. N.
Tel: 206-632-6695
This fun, young boutique is full of sexy, bias-cut reversible dresses, tees, tanks, and jeans.

Buffalo Exchange
4530 University Way N.E.
Tel: 206-545-0175
(See Flagstaff, AZ, listing)

Fini
86 Pine St.
Tel: 206-443-0563
A discriminating collection of handbags, gloves, jewelry, hats, belts, scarves, hair ornaments, and leather goods.

Les Amis
3420 Evanston Ave. N.
Tel: 206-632-2877
Everything in this store is arranged by color, and the goodies—handbags, perfume, jewelry, and lingerie—are scattered about.

Mario's
1513 Sixth Ave.
Tel: 206-622-6161
Expect all the heavy hitters at Seattle's store for serious fashion.

Nordstrom
500 Pine St.
Tel: 206-628-2111
Seattle is the home base for this national chain, legendary for service and shoes.

Olive
1633 Sixth Ave.
Tel: 206-254-1310
This "general store" houses upscale, individually owned boutiques including a sexy shoe shop, and boutiques with cutting-edge clothing.

Olivine Atelier
5344 Ballard Ave. N.W.
Tel: 206-706-4188
Girly-girls will be fully satisfied with the dresses, jeans, lingerie, handbags, and cosmetics here.

Pearl
310 N.E. 65th St.
Tel: 206-729-1149
Pick up funky wallets, frilly Mexican festival sandals, and items for the beach at this shop.

Ped
1115 First Ave.
Tel: 206-292-1767
Seattle's coolest shoe store.

Powder Room
101 Stewart St., #101
Tel: 206-374-0060
Sexy styles that won't break the bank fill the racks here.

Tininha's Boutique
2612 N.E. 55th St.
Tel: 206-985-6772
Ultra-sexy Brazilian bikinis in more than 200 styles, plus Brazilian lingerie, and beach accessories.

Trendy Wendy
211 Broadway E.
Tel: 206-322-6642
Always stocked up-to-the-minute styles, this shop carries clothing, shoes, lingerie, and handbags.

Tulip
1201 First Ave.
Tel: 206-223-1790
This laid-back boutique has a warm, inviting feel, and stock of each season's key items.

WISCONSIN
MADISON
Bop
222 W. Gorham St.
Tel: 608-255-2570
This established shop caters to a
college clientele.

CANADA
ALBERTA
CALGARY
Holt Renfrew
751 3rd St. S.W.
Tel: 403-269-7341
This posh department store has
some avant-garde items thrown into
its mix; the handbags section is the
real draw.

EDMONTON
Holt Renfrew
10180 101st St.
Tel: 780-425-5300
(See Calgary, Alberta, listing)

BRITISH COLUMBIA
VANCOUVER
Aritzia
1110 Robson St.
Tel: 604-684-3251
These locally owned clothing
boutiques sell garments at the
pinnacle of trendiness.

Atomic Model
1036 Mainland St.
Tel: 604-688-9989
This boutique carries sought-after
clothing lines such as Development.

Bruce
1038 Alberni St.
Tel: 604-688-8802
The downtown boutique to make
sure to hit; it carries hard-to-find
labels, and features an in-store
eyewear boutique.

Eugene Choo
3683 Main St.
Tel: 604-873-8874
Customized clothing and accessories,
with local and international brands.

Holt Renfrew
633 Granville St.
Tel: 604-681-3121
(See Calgary, Alberta, listing)

Kawabata-Ya
437 W. Hastings
Tel: 604-806-0020
One of our very favorite vintage boutiques—organized, well-lighted, with
an amazing selection of wearables.

The Block
350 W. Cordova St.
Tel: 604-685-8885
This loft-size space sells everything
from bowling bags to cords to
tweedy fitted jackets.

True Value Vintage
710 Robson St.
Tel: 604-685-5403
This vintage store has good prices on
lots of leather jackets, outerwear,
and sweaters.

ONTARIO
OTTAWA
Holt Renfrew
240 Sparks St.
Tel: 613-238-2200
(See Calgary, Alberta, listing)

TORONTO
Augustina
138 Cumberland St.
Tel: 416-922-4248
This boutique stocks a small but
exquisite selection of luxe shoes,
lingerie, bathing suits, scarves,
handbags, and hats.

Boudoir
990 Queen St. W.
Tel: 416-535-6600
This vintage store sells everything
from the apparel to the pieces that
display them.

Cabaret
672 Queen St. W.
Tel: 416-504-7126
This vintage shop has glamorous
'20s gowns, retro-chic '60s dresses,
and a stellar collection of hats and
jewelry.

Holt Renfrew
50 Bloor St. W.
Tel: 416-922-2333
and
25 The West Mall
Etobicoke
Tel: 416-621-9900
and
3401 Dufferin at Highway 401
Tel: 416-789-5377

(See Calgary, Alberta, listing)
Icii
99 Yorkville Ave.
Tel: 416-925-3380
Mostly Japanese and Belgian lines
are carried here.

Jumas
655 Collège St.
Tel: 416-530-0207
The owner of this slightly upscale
destination has impeccable taste and
a gift for mixing edgy pieces.

Lululemon Athletica
734 Queen St. W.
Tel: 416-703-1399
The yoga-inspired clothes at this
sunny shop easily go from studio to
street.

Maxi
575 Danforth Ave.
Tel: 416-461-6686
A source for sleek trousers, dramatic
suits, and the latest tops and skirts.

Peachy Fresh
111 Yorkville Ave., upstairs
Tel: 416-513-9884
A collective founded by a dozen
local designers, this whimsical oasis
sells an eclectic mix of clothing,
accessories, and jewelry.

Preloved
613 Queen St. W.
Tel: 416-504-8704
This line of reconstructed vintage
tees and denim is a huge hit all
across Canada.

Propaganda
686 Yonge St.
Tel: 416-961-0555
Affordable jewelry, belts, clothes, and
accessories by Canadian designers.

Swaby
898 Danforth Ave.
Tel: 416-367-1333
The feminine and romantic clothes
sold here include '40s-style
wool crepe suits, ruffled tanks, and
eyelet boxers.

Sim & Jones
388 Collège St.
Tel: 416-920-2573
The garments offer function with a
twist at this bohemian clothing and
home décor shop.

Wenches & Rogues
110 Yorkville Ave.

Tel: 416-920-8959
Local actors and artists swear by this
well-established store.

QUEBEC
MONTREAL
Holt Renfrew
1300 Sherbrooke St. W.
Tel: 514-842-5111
and
2305 Chemin Rockland
Ville Mont-Royal
Tel: 514-738-3500
(See Calgary, Alberta, listing)

James
4910 Sherbrooke W.
Westmount
Tel: 514-369-0700
One of Quebec's best, this boutique
stocks ahead-of-the-curve labels
and great beachy stuff.

Lola & Emily
3475 Blvd. St. Laurent
Tel: 514-288-7598
One of Montreal's best, this store
offers the perfect mix of funky and
functional clothing.

Mona Moore
1446 Sherbrooke W.
Tel: 514-842-0662
This footwear shop is filled with the
sharpest of shoes.

Mosquito
1651 St. Catherine W.
Tel: 514-939-6793
and
1455 Peel
Tel: 514-286-5244
and
3521 Blvd. St. Laurent
Tel: 514-288-6839
This trio of stores sells progressive
lines like Development and Paul &
Friends, along with crowd-pleaser
Miss Sixty.

Preloved
4832 Blvd. St. Laurent
Tel: 514-499-9898
(See Toronto, Ontario, listing)

QUEBEC CITY
Holt Renfrew
2452 Blvd. Laurier
Sainte-Foy
Tel: 418-656-6783
(See Calgary, Alberta, listing)

bluefly.com

Save $20 on a purchase of $100 or more by entering code "LUCKYBOOK" at checkout at www.bluefly.com.

Offer is for a limited time only and ends at 11:59 PM ET on December 31, 2003. Offer is subject to a minimum merchandise purchase of $100 and may be used only once. For additional details and restrictions, see the HELP section of www.bluefly.com.

save
$20

underglam, inc.

Save 20% at www.underglam.com by entering "luckymag" at checkout.

save
20%

benefit

Spend $50 and receive a free Glamourette. Go to www.benefitcosmetics.com/luckybook. Coy or Fickle Glamourette Ensemble Only. While supplies last.

save
$50

URBAN OUTFITTERS

Save 20% on a purchase of $50 or more at all Urban Outfitters stores, at www.urbanoutfitters.com, and through the Urban Outfitters catalog. Show this page at Urban Outfitters stores; enter "luckymag" at checkout in the promotional code section of www.urbanoutfitters.com; or to shop from the Urban Outfitters catalog, call 800-282-2200 to order, and mention Lucky Breaks. Offer expires 12/31/03.

save
20%

NINE WEST

Save $20 on a purchase of $100 or more at Nine West Specialty stores and at www.ninewest.com. To redeem the offer, show this page in stores or use promotion code "NOVLUCKY" at checkout online. Valid only in the United States. One time only offer. May not be combined with any other offers. Not valid at Nine West Outlet Stores. Not valid on previous purchases or on gift certificates. Not redeemable for cash or credit.

Store use only: Scan item, <F2>, <F2>, <F1>, <F5>, Code 020090103, $20, complete transaction. UPC Locator Code: Your 4-digit store # + NOV3LUC STS CORPORATE CODE 020090103

save
$20

SPECIAL THANKS TO THE FOLLOWING DESIGNERS, WHOSE CLOTHES AND ACCESSORIES WERE USED IN THIS BOOK:

A

A.B.S. by Allen Schwartz
Adrienne Vittadini
Aerosoles
Agnès B.
Alessandro dell'Acqua
Ambika Bikini
American Apparel
American Eagle Outfitters
Andrew Marc
Ani Olson
Anna Sui
Anne Klein
Ann Taylor
Anya Hindmarch
A.P.C.
Arden B.
Arizona
Ashley Paige
Asp
Autumn Cashmere
A/X Armani Exchange

B

Baccarat
Badgley Mischka
Bally
Banana Republic
BCBG Max Azria
BDG
Beautiful People
Bebe
Bell & Ross
Bell by Alicia Bell
Beth Bowley
Betsey Johnson
Beverly Feldman
Bijoux Givenchy
Birkett
Bloom
Blue Cult
Blue Plate

Bodyhints
Boucher
Bramasolé
Bravo-Banks
Brooklyn Handknit
Bruno Magli
Built by Wendy
Buoy
Burberry
Buz Jones
Buzz by Jane Fox

C

Cacharel
Calvin Klein
Calypso St. Barth
Carla Mancini
Cartier
Catherine Malandrino
Celine
Cesare Paciotti
Chaiken
Chanel
Charles David
Cherry Pie
Chinese Laundry
Christian Dior
Christian Lacroix
Christine Ganeaux
Claudette
Clogmaster
Club Monaco
Coach
Cole Haan
Corey Lynn Calter
Cosabella
Courrèges
C.P. Company
CYDWOQ
Cynthia Rowley

D

D & Doyle
Danier
Daryl K.
DDC Lab
Delia's
Dessous Dessus
Diane von Furstenberg
Diesel
Dockers
Dolce & Gabbana
Dollhouse
Dolma
Domani
Donald J. Pliner
Donna Karan
Dooney & Bourke
Dosa

E

Earl Jean
Eberjey
Edmundo Castillo
Edward An
Elie Tahari
Elizabeth Gillett
Ella Moss
Ellen Tracy
Emanuel Ungaro
Emma Hope
Erica Tanov
Escada
Etienne Aigner
Express

F

Faded Glory
Fendi
Fever Jeans
Foley + Corinna
For Joseph

Fortunoff
Franchi
Frankie B.
Fred Leighton
French Connection
Fubu Bags
Furla

G

Gap
Gigi
Gina
Girdle
Gnipoos
Graham Kandiah
Gucci
Guess?
Gunmetal

H

Hadu
HaléBob
Hanes
Hanro of Switzerland
Hat Attack
Havaianas
Hedra Prue
Helmut Lang
Hermès
Hollywould
Honora
Hugo Boss
Hype

I

ICB
Il Bisonte
Inca

J

Jaeger
James
James Perse
Jantzen
J. Crew
Jethro
Jill Michelle
Jill Stuart
J.J. Hat Center
Jockey
Johnny Farah
Joie
Jones New York
Joseph
Juicy Couture
Juliana Rosa Cho
Julie Brown
Justin

K

Kaki Daniels
Katayone Adeli
K.C. Designs
Keds
Kenneth Cole
Khurana
Killah
Kim Davis London

L

La Blanca by Rod Beattie
La Cosa
Lacoste
Lambertson Truex
Lands' End
Language
Laundry by Shelli Segal
Laura Urbinati
Lauren Moffatt
Lemon Twist
Leslie Han
Letarte by Lisa Cabrinha
Levi's
Linea Nervenkitt
Lisa Curran Swim
Liz Claiborne
L Space
Lotta
Louis Vuitton
Louison
Loulie at Apropo
L.L. Bean
Lulu Guinness

M

Mad Bomber
Malia Mills
Malibu Dream Girl
Manolo Blahnik

Marc Jacobs
Margo Hotston for Bondi Bathers
Martin
MaxMara
Maxstudio.com
Maxx
Mayle
Mercy Jones
Michael Kors
Michael Stars
Michelle K. Footwear
Miguelina
Miki P.
Milk Fed
Milly
Mimco
Missoni
Miu Miu
Mon Petit Oiseau
Monsac
Moschino
Mossimo at Target
M.R.S.

N

Nancy Bacich
Nanette Lepore
Naturalizer
Nautica
Necessary Objects
New York & Company
New York Transit
Newport News
Nicole Farhi
Nicole Miller
Nike
Nina
Nine West
Norma Kamali

O

O Maillots de Bain
Old Navy
On Gossamer
OndadeMar
Only Hearts by Helena Stuart
OP
Opera by Sueli Costa
Oscar de la Renta

P

Parallel
Patty Lynn Poolwear
Paul & Joe
Petit Bateau
Philip Treacy
Philosophy di Alberta Ferretti
Phyllis Leibowitz
Pierre Hardy
Pixie Yates

Poker Face
Polo Jeans Co. Ralph Lauren
Pompeii
Prada
Puma

R

Rafé
Rampage
Randell Dodge
Rebecca Norman
Rebecca Taylor
Reyes
Richard Tyler
Richelieu
Riveted by Lee
R.J. Graziano
Roberta Chiarella
Robert Danes
Robin Piccone
Ro
Rosa Ferrer
Route 66
Ruth

S

Sabrina Nadal
Sacco
Salinas
Salvatore Ferragamo
Sara Lasier
Saucony
See by Chloé
Self Esteem
Sergio Rossi
Seven
Shay Todd
Shin Choi
Shoshanna
Sigerson Morrison
Sisley
Six Fourteen
Sky
Spiegel
St. Vincent
Stella McCartney
Stephen Dweck
Steve Madden
Streets Ahead
Stuart Weitzman
Sundance
Sven

T

Talisman
Ten Thousand Things
The Limited
Theory
The Sak Elliott Lucca
Tibi

Tiffany & Co.
Tocca
Tod's
Tom K. Nguyen
Tommy Hilfiger
Tono su Tono
To the Max!
Tova Celine
Tracy Reese
Tree
Tres Flores
Trina Turk
Trio New York
Triple 5 Soul
Tyr Sport, Inc.

U

United Colors of Benetton
Urban Outfitters

V

Vanessa Bruno
Versace
Via Spiga
Victoria's Secret
Vitamin A by Amahlia Stevens
Vivienne Tam

W

Wacoal
Wet Seal
White + Warren
Whiting & Davis
William B.
Wilsons Leather

X

Xanthe Bags
XOXO

Y

Yves Saint Laurent

Z

Zero Maria Cornejo

This book was produced by Melcher Media, Inc., 124 West 13th Street, New York, NY 10011, www.melcher.com

PUBLISHER: Charles Melcher
EDITOR: Lia Ronnen
PRODUCTION DIRECTOR: Andrea Hirsh
PUBLISHING MANAGER: Bonnie Eldon
DESIGN: Ph.D

STYLIST: Liz Kiernan
STYLIST: Sharon Anderson
PHOTO RESEARCHER: Sue Hostetler
EDITORIAL ASSISTANT: Ritsuko Okumura
EDITORIAL ASSISTANT: Katie Claypoole

SPECIAL THANKS: Rick Levine
THANKS: Anne Johnston Albert, Leah Ansel, Jackie Baker, Meredith Barnett, Duncan Bock, David Brown, Carolyn Clark, Lisa Connelly, Max Dickstein, Margo Donohue, Carlota Espinosa, Liana Fredley, Miguelina Gambaccini, Barrie Gillies, Gigi Guerra, Ethan Hauser, Michael Hodgson, Shayla Hunter, Elizabeth Johnson, Ashley Kennedy, Simon Kon, Karyn Kloumann, Eleanor Lembo, Fiona Lennon, Gene Linett, Shoshanna Lonstein, Jessica Marshall, Lauren Marino, Stef McDonald, James Morris, Michael Morse, Allison Murray, Carol Kono Noble, Clive Piercy, Marlien Rentmeester, Alberto del Rosal, Jeffrey Schad, William Shinker, Donna Sollecito, Andrea Todd, James Truman, Ann Marie Tullo, Allyson Waterman, Debra Weintraub, Brooke Williams, Shân Willis, and Megan Worman.

THANKS TO THE FOLLOWING PHOTOGRAPHERS, WHOSE PHOTOS APPEAR THROUGHOUT THIS BOOK: Paul Armbruster, Chris Bartlett, David Bashaw, Davies + Starr, Coppola + Grande, Cathy Crawford, Squire Fox, Sebastian Gollings, Denise Grasso, Devon Jarvis, Spencer Jones, Darrin Haddad, Gregor Halenda, Todd Huffman, David Lawrence, Patrick McMullen, Peter Medilek, Jens Mortensen, Francesco Mosto, Jason Nocito, Eric Ogden, Darryl Patterson, Ron Reeves, David Roth, Jeffrey Schad, Josephine Schiele, Zane White, James Worrell, and Andrew Zuckerman.